WEAPON

THE M4 CARBINE

CHRIS McNAB
Series Editor Martin Pegler

Illustrated by Johnny Shumate & Alan Gilliland

OSPREY PUBLISHING
Bloomsbury Publishing Plc
Kemp House, Chawley Park, Cumnor Hill, Oxford OX2 9PH, UK
1385 Broadway, 5th Floor, New York, NY 10018, USA
E-mail: info@ospreypublishing.com
www.ospreypublishing.com

OSPREY is a trademark of Osprey Publishing Ltd

First published in Great Britain in 2021

A catalog record for this book is available from the British
Library.

ISBN: PB 9781472842275; eBook 9781472842282;
ePDF 9781472842251; XML 9781472842268

21 22 23 24 25   10 9 8 7 6 5 4 3 2 1

Index by Rob Munro
Typeset by PDQ Digital Media Solutions, Bungay, UK
Printed and bound in India by Replika Press Private Ltd.

To find out more about our authors and books visit
www.ospreypublishing.com. Here you will find extracts, author
interviews, details of forthcoming events and the option to sign
up for our newsletter.

Acknowledgments

I would like to thank Vedant Tiwari for his useful insights into
the military experience of handling the M4 Carbine, and also
Alan Pike for his much-appreciated assistance with internal
technical details of the M4A1 cutaway in this book. Thanks to
Raytheon ELCAN (sights) and Armament Technology Inc.
(reticles) for their kind permission to reproduce the reticle images
for the Specter® DR1-4× and Specter® OS4× on page 25. Thanks
also to John Bailey of EOTech for permission to reproduce, on
page 27, the EOTech 0 reticle from the EOTech Holographic
Weapon Sight. Thanks also go to Bob Hurley, for opening up
new contacts and for being so customarily generous with his
time, and to Nick Reynolds of Osprey Publishing, for fine-tuning
the book ready for publication.

Front cover, above: This M4A1 carbine has been fitted with the
M26 12-gauge Modular Accessory Shotgun System (MASS). As
well as firing door-breaching rounds and regular shot, the MASS
can fire less-lethal munitions. (Photo courtesy of PEO Soldier/
Wikimedia/Public Domain)
Front cover, below: Specialist Nicholas Haney, from the
23d Infantry Regiment, 172nd Stryker Brigade Combat Team,
patrols Mosul, Iraq, December 8, 2005. (http://www.army.mil/
Wikimedia/Public Domain)
Title-page photo: The M4 carbine is one of the world's most
common weapons among law-enforcement personnel and SWAT-
type teams. Here US Border Patrol trainees fire M4 carbines
during a weapons training class at the US Border Patrol Academy
in Artesia, New Mexico on August 3, 2017. (John Moore/Getty
Images)

CONTENTS

INTRODUCTION

The M4A1 carbine, shown here with the optional carrying handle fitted to the top rail. This weapon has the six-position "waffle stock," which unlike the classic CAR-15-type stock has a sling mount on the bottom. The cut-out sections of the stock reduce the weapon's weight. (Jackolmos/Wikimedia/CC BY-SA 3.0)

This book is a contribution to a library reflecting divided opinions. Much like the 5.56mm M16 rifle from which it is derived, the M4 carbine is something of a lightning rod for polarized arguments. To give a sense of the gulf in opinions involved, two magazine articles can be cited. First, the January/February 2015 issue of *The Atlantic* ran a lengthy article by Robert H. Scales, a retired US Army major general and former commandant of the Army War College (Scales 2015). Entitled "Gun Trouble," the article squarely criticizes both the M16 and the M4, calling them "badly flawed" and pointing to what Scales alleges are critical problems at the heart of the operating system itself. For Scales, it appears little short of criminal that US troops go into action armed with the M4.

In vivid contrast, a 2019 article in *The National Interest* nails a very different set of colors to the mast, the title alone making the author's position all too clear: "M4 Carbine: this rifle is so good that the U.S. Army can't lose a shootout." The article's author, Kyle Mizokami, acknowledges that the M4 is not perfect, but he nevertheless praises it as a sound, battle-winning weapon. He addresses some of Scales' concerns by pointing to military field reports from Afghanistan and Iraq, reports that largely express the confidence of front-line troops in the M4 and M4A1. For Mizokami, front-line approbation trumps any technical debates.

In between these two opinions, there are many more that mold the debate, exhibiting varying degrees of moderation. This book will attempt its own negotiation of the arguments, working toward as balanced a conclusion as possible, while also chronicling the technical evolution, combat history, and performance of the weapon. As we shall see, any evaluation of a weapon's worth must crucially include the human factor in the study, for a firearm is not a standalone device: in both its combat performance and its reliability, it relies to a critical degree on the handling skills, discipline, and mechanical intelligence of its user. Therefore, an evaluation of the M4/M4A1 implicitly involves some level of evaluation of the troops who carry it.

What we cannot argue with, however, is the enormous production and distribution success of the M4/M4A1. Since its entry into service in 1994, the M4/M4A1 (alongside full-length M16 rifles) has been one of the standard – and in front-line combat units, increasingly preferred – firearms of the US armed forces, with hundreds of thousands in use. Outside the M4/M4A1's homeland, furthermore, the weapon has been adopted by more than 60 countries to greater or lesser degrees. One thing critics of the M4/M4A1 cannot dismiss is the achievement of its widespread adoption.

Volume production and widespread service are not, to be fair, always a guarantee of a quality firearm – think the British 5.56mm L85A1 Rifle before the Heckler & Koch upgrade, and indeed the early days of the M16's adoption in the mid-1960s. There can also be a heavy dose of politics and economics behind arms deals, with purchases of specific arms often part of complex horse-trading between countries. What is crucial is that the M4/M4A1 has seen service during one of the most militarily active periods of post-1945 history, including the two exceptionally lengthy wars in Afghanistan (2001–present) and Iraq (2003–present). In these conflicts, the M4/M4A1 has been tested to destruction, sometimes literally so, in the hands of both regular infantry and also by Special

This classic image shows US Navy SEALs training with Colt Commando/XM177s in the mid-1980s. In many ways, it is the US SOF community that has pioneered or influenced the development of modern carbine weapons in the US military. (JO1 (SS) Peter D. Sundberg/PD-USGov-Military-Navy)

A US Army Delta Force operator armed with a Colt Model 723 M16A2 carbine, one of the carbine iterations that preceded the arrival of the M4 carbine, performs VIP protection duty for General Norman Schwarzkopf during the First Gulf War (1990–91). Delta Force operators found that the carbine's short effective range (compared to that of M16 rifles) was a limitation during the desert operations of Operation *Desert Storm.* (US Army Staff Sergeant Dean W. Wagner/Wikimedia/Public Domain)

Operations Forces (SOF), for whom the carbine was often the weapon of choice. The development of advanced packages of tactical accessories for the M4/M4A1 – including tactical day and night optics, flashlights, laser/infrared designators and illuminators, adjustable stocks, optional forends and front grips, and underbarrel grenade launchers and shotguns – have given the M4/M4A1 the "modularity" that is a hallmark of the latest generations of military rifles and carbines. The combat testing of both the core weapon and its modular features has been intense and relentless over the last two decades, including by international users, and has been the subject of close scrutiny by military officials and by front-line troops whose lives depend upon their firearms.

The last point is particularly important. We should remember that around the year 2000, the internet was transformed by the introduction of high-speed broadband wifi. This technology led to an explosion of communication and sharing, including among the serving and veteran military communities and between the military, media, and public. The outputs of these conversations, official and informal, are readily available. In short, we certainly have enough statistical and observational data to develop an informed opinion as to the value and capabilities of the M4/M4A1. If anything, we possibly have a surfeit of information; the challenge is to make sense of all the competing voices and to find clear lines of conclusion. One thing we can say at the outset, however, is that the M4/M4A1 has been one of the defining firearms of the first decades of the 21st century. In the hands of tens of thousands of men and women on the world's front lines, it has been far more than the subject of academic study; it has been an essential tool of combat.

DEVELOPMENT
Progressive evolution

The first carbines based on the M16 rifle emerged almost as quickly as the rifle itself, in the form of the 5.56mm CAR-15 (Colt Automatic Rifle) family of weapons. The story of these carbines is almost a book-length narrative in itself (a summary is provided in Rottman 2011: 30–32), but

The GUU-5/P was a US Air Force variant within the CAR-15 family. It removed the short barrels and flash suppressors of the GAU-5A and fitted a 14.5in barrel with a 1-in-12in rifling twist. (US Air Force/ Wikimedia/Public Domain)

Three US Army Rangers participate in a training exercise in 1986. The Ranger in the foreground is armed with an M16A1 (Model 653) carbine, with retractable buttstock and forward assist. (DOD/Wikimedia/Public Domain)

it is most strongly defined by the Colt Commando/XM177 and the US Air Force variant, the GAU-5, with both these types further divided into sub-variants.

The CAR-15 weapons had much commonality in terms of their operating mechanism with the M16/M16A1 rifles, but their radical reduction in barrel length – between 10in and 14.5in – and the fitting of telescopic stocks resulted in a portable piece of firepower ideally suited to SOF use. Thus the CAR-15s not only delivered close-quarters firepower throughout the Vietnam War, in the hands of SEALs, US Army Special Forces, Rangers, and other elites, but also served well beyond into the 1970s, 1980s, and 1990s, in all manner of operational contexts. The degree to which they gave good service is open to discussion, however.

Reducing the barrel length significantly, particularly at the shortest ends of the scale, created a host of issues with muzzle blast, noise, recoil, and parts failure. A key problem stemmed from the shortening of the distance between the gas port and the end of the barrel, which significantly reduced "dwell time" – the interval of time in which the bullet acts as a plug for the gases in the barrel before it exits the muzzle. This reduced duration meant that the gas system and the bolt-carrier group all functioned under extremely high pressures at the moment the bolt unlocked, which put the system under heavy strain. Solving this and several other issues would call on the expertise of Colt's carbine engineers for several decades. This process did mean, however, that when they arrived at the M4 carbine they had a significant body of engineering experience behind them.

Photographed in the early 1990s in the Persian Gulf, a US Air Force security policeman puts in some range time with his Colt Commando/XM177. Note the absence of the forward assist used on the AR-15 rifles and the presence of the bulbous flash-hider, the latter imperative to control the short-barrel carbine's blast and flash. (Tech. Sgt. Marvin Lynchard/Wikimedia/Public Domain)

THE REQUIREMENT

The need for a standardized carbine in the US Army, not just limited CAR-15 types issued to the SOF community, was defined in the first half of the 1980s. In 1983, the Army Development and Employment Agency (ADEA) was created to explore innovations in equipment and tactics. A major vehicle for its investigations was the 9th Infantry Division, which was intended to test the new High Technology Motorized Division (HTMD) concept. One of the ideas emerging (in April 1983) from the 9th Infantry Division was the requirement, under the Quick Reaction Program (QRP), for a 5.56mm carbine, to replace the .30 M1 carbines and submachine guns then in service, the new weapon to be used by vehicle-mounted and dismounted front-line support troops. The most logical candidate identified in the proposal was the XM177E2, which had an 11.5in barrel and the upper and lower receivers of the M16A1. Improving the furniture and fitting a barrel with a 1-in-7in barrel twist rate – suitable for both the M193 and the newer M855 5.56×45mm cartridges – would bring the weapon up to the 9th Infantry Division's requirements. After analysis by the Armament Research and Development Center (ARDC) in June 1983, however, the approach was changed. The ARDC wanted a new weapon based upon the M16A2, but with a 14.5in barrel. The change in specification was accepted by the 9th Infantry Division, and in January 1984 the future firearm was designated the XM4 within the QRP; development was officially approved by the US Army the following month. In June 1985, the Picatinny Arsenal in New Jersey was awarded contract DAAA21-85-C-0192 to produce 40 XM4 prototypes.

The journey of the new weapon to fruition was a fiscally and politically frustrating process. By the end of the 1985 it was a joint US Army/US Marine Corps program, but the following year the Army withdrew its funding. The Marine Corps subsequently provided much of the project finance, with generally low interest from the Army (at least for the moment). Nevertheless, in January 1987 the Marine Corps approved the weapon for service, although it ordered only 892 carbines for FY 1987, and on the penultimate day of the same month the recalcitrant Army type-classified it as "carbine, 5.56mm, M4."

CONFIGURATION

A central requirement of the Colt M4 development program was to have maximum parts commonality with the M16A2 rifle, to aid logistics and maintenance. This Colt achieved, with *c.*80 percent parts commonality. Like the M16 rifles, the M4 is a gas-operated 5.56mm weapon using the AR-15's direct-impingement, rotating-bolt operating mechanism. The *c.*20 percent parts difference between the M4 and the M16A2 has some significant aspects to it, however. Here we will note some of the core changes in the M4 as it emerged into service, not only compared to the M16A2, but also to its XM177 and GAU-5 predecessors.

The carbines of the Vietnam War up to the mid-1980s used two generations of collapsible stock, the first something like a fixed stock but with the length adjusted by a lever in the butt pad, the second a polymer-coated aluminum type with position adjustment. The first type of stock to be fitted to the M4 was a third-generation collapsible type introduced in 1985; made purely of plastic, it was called the "fiberlite stock." Initially this stock had only two positions – fully closed or fully extended – but later versions featured four-position adjustment. The defining M4/M4A1 stock, however, came with the fourth-generation type, known as the "M4 stock" or "six-position stock" on account of its additional adjustability. This stock is primarily recognizable by the multitude of cut-out sections and recesses on the side, hence it is also known as the "waffle stock."

One of the problems associated with the earlier Colt carbines was the buildup of extreme heat around the barrel and forend. Colt's lead engineer Henry Tatro therefore designed a new **handguard** with double heat shields for the M4.

Turning to **rail and iron sights**, the M4 was initially issued with the carrying handle integral to the upper receiver. From *c*.1995, however, the M4 had a flat-top receiver fitted with a MIL-STD-1913 rail. The carrying handle thus became an optional fitting, often ignored in favor of optical sights and other tactical accessories. One point to note about the carrying handle is that with the M4 the rear diopter sight was only adjustable up to 600m (656yd), as opposed to the 800m (875yd) of the M16A2, on account of the M4's reduced range because of its shorter barrel. The absence of the carrying handle did not mean that the gun went without iron sights, however: rail-mountable backup iron sights (BUIS) were available, made by companies such as ARMS, Knight's Armament, and MaTech.

The M4 introduced what was known as the "F-Marked" **front sight base**, which raised the front sight a little higher to align it with the sights integral to the carrying handle, which now themselves sat a little higher once the carrying handle was fitted to the MIL-STD-1913 rail. Alternatively, some sights' configurations simply raised the height of the front sight post to compensate.

In most ways, the M4's **bolt-carrier group** was identical with that of the M16A2, but with the important exception of the extractor system. Because of the shortened gas tube configuration described above, the spent cartridge case was, at the point of its extraction from the chamber, under greater gas pressures and therefore more stubbornly resistant to extraction. Colt made the entire extractor system far more robust, with an extra spring coil for the extractor spring to improve reliability. The system was still under intense strain, however, and US Special Operations

A US Navy sailor assembles the bolt of an M4 carbine, the angle of the photograph clearly showing the bolt locking lugs and the extractor claw (at the 3 o'clock position on the bolt head), and the ejector (at the 9 o'clock position). (MC1 Michelle L. Turner/Public domain photograph from defenseimagery.mil)

Command (SOCOM) operators putting their weapons through hard operational use in Afghanistan and Iraq would subsequently fit a rubber O-ring around the extractor spring to increase the extraction force by a factor of four. Later this improvised measure would become standard fitting on the M4 and M4A1.

The **receiver extension** was extended so that a four-position collapsible stock could be fitted (the GAU-5 and XM177 carbines only had two-position stocks, for fully open or fully closed positions). The reason for the greater flexibility in ergonomics was that the modern soldier is often heavily clad in body armor, and thus has to adjust the length of pull (the distance between the trigger and the end of the buttstock) to allow for the additional depth of clothing and equipment.

On the XM177 the **receiver extension nut** was adjustable at a single point via the use of a wrench, but the M4 had a new four-point locking system that was easier to adjust.

The **buffer** was a particularly important modification on the M4. Because of its shortened gas system and the higher pressures produced, the M4 had a higher rate of fire than the M16A2: up to 950rd/min as opposed to about c.800rd/min for the rifle. This faster speed resulted in two main issues. First, the bolt carrier recoiled off the buffer quicker and returned to battery at higher speeds – a motion that sometimes resulted in "bolt bounce," when the carrier hit the barrel extension and bounced back a fraction, just enough to prevent the firing pin from striking the primer of the next cartridge and resulting in a stoppage. Second, the speed of the forward stroke caused problems with loading the new M855 cartridge, which is slightly longer and sharper in profile than the M193 cartridge. When the M855 was being chambered, the nose of the bullet sometimes struck either the chamber or even the receiver, resulting in misfeeds.

Two solutions were implemented to solve these problems. The first was to install a new "H" buffer, which had two steel weights and one heavier tungsten weight inside. The extra weight inside the buffer slowed the

COLT M4 AND M4A1 CARBINE SPECIFICATIONS

The following data is adapted from US Army (1991) TM 9-1005-319-23&P, *Unit and Direct Support Maintenance Manual* (for the M16A2, M4 and M4A1), pp. 27–28.

SPECIFICATIONS		US customary	Metric
Weight			
Carbine, M4/M4A1, without magazine and sling		6lb 7oz	2.91kg
Rifle, M16A2, without magazine and sling		7lb 8oz	3.40kg
Sling, adjustable		4oz	0.11kg
Empty magazine		4oz	0.11kg
Loaded magazine		1lb 1oz	0.48kg
Carbine, M4/M4A1, with sling and loaded magazine		7lb 12oz	3.51kg
Rifle, M16A2, with sling and loaded magazine		8lb 13oz	4.00kg
Bayonet-knife M7		10.5oz	0.30kg
Scabbard M10		5oz	0.14kg
Length			
Carbine with compensator, buttstock extended		33.0in	83.82cm
Carbine with compensator, buttstock closed		29.75in	75.57cm
Rifle with compensator		39.63in	100.66cm
Barrel	Carbine	14.5in	36.83cm
	Rifle	20in	50.8cm
Barrel with compensator	Carbine	15.5in	39.37cm
	Rifle	21in	53.34cm
Mechanical features			
Rifling		Right-hand twist six grooves, one turn in 7in (17.78cm)	
Method of operation		direct gas	
Type of breech mechanism		rotating bolt	
Method of feeding		Magazine	
Cooling		Air	
Trigger pull	M16A2 & M4	5.5–9.5lb	2.49–4.31kg
	M4A1	5.5–8.5lb	2.49–3.86kg
Ammunition			
Caliber		0.223	5.56mm
Type		ball, blank, dummy, and tracer	
Firing characteristics			
Muzzle velocity (approximate)	Carbine	2,970ft/sec	905.85m/sec
	Rifle	3,100ft/sec	945.5m/sec
Chamber pressure		52,000psi	358,540kPa
Cyclic rate of fire (approximate)	Carbine	700–970rd/min	
	Rifle	700–900rd/min	
Maximum rate of fire			
Semiautomatic		45rd/min	
Burst		90rd/min	
Sustained rate of fire		12–15rd/min	
Maximum range (approximate)		3,938yd	3,600m
Maximum effective range			
Individual/point targets	Carbine	547yd	500m
	Rifle	602yd	550m
Area targets	Carbine	650yd	600m
	Rifle	875yd	800m

return stroke of the bolt, curing the bolt bounce and also giving the M855 cartridge time to feed properly. As an additional remedy for the feed problems, the M4 was fitted with extended **feed ramps**, giving the M855 a longer and smoother transition into the chamber.

The **trigger mechanism** of the M4 was largely that of the M16A2, with Safe – Semi – Burst (three-round-burst) modes of fire. On the M4, however, the notches in the three-round-burst cam were cut a little deeper than those on the rifle, to prevent what were referred to as "non-conforming bursts," i.e. firing more than three shots.

PRODUCTION AND CONTROVERSY

The first decade of the M4's existence was a troubled one, as the weapon became caught up in political and industrial wrangling. At first, the M4 garnered limited attention from the US Army; the US Marine Corps was the principal early adopter. In the late 1980s and early 1990s, however, the Army's interest in acquiring a carbine was reignited, aided by the lessons learned during the First Gulf War. In May and July 1993, the Army finally awarded its own production contracts to Colt for M4 carbines, with a subsequent contract for M4A1 carbines – mainly for use by SOCOM operators – awarded in February 1994.

Before going on to consider the M4A1, and the subsequent evolution of both the M4 and M4A1, they should be set in an important contractual context, one that had an influence on the development of both weapons. To set the scene, in 1967 the US Army purchased a license from Colt for the M16 technical data package (TDP). A TDP, as defined by the Defense Security Cooperation Agency, "Normally includes technical design and manufacturing information sufficient to enable the construction or manufacture of a defense item component modification, or to enable the performance of certain maintenance or production processes. It may include blueprints, drawings, plans, or instructions that can be used or adapted for use in the design, production, manufacture, or maintenance of defense items or technology" (Defense Security Cooperation Agency).

The licensing of the M16 TDP meant that the Department of Defense (DOD) could "second source" M16 weapons and parts. In the context of the M4, however, the US Army did not license the TDP, and the M4 was developed outside the 1967 agreement with Colt. In early 1996, the Naval Surface Warfare Center-Crane (NSWC-Crane) in Indiana requested the M4 TDP from the US Army's Rock Island Arsenal, in relation to the acquisition of accessories for the SOPMOD kit program (see below). In the process, NSWC-Crane distributed the TDP to 21 vendors, but without Colt's knowledge or approval. The DOD, alerted to the problem by an angered Colt, quickly withdrew the TDPs, but the situation produced a great deal of heat and light, especially as the Belgian firearms manufacturer, Fabrique Nationale d'Herstal (FN Herstal), one of the recipients of the TDP, subsequently submitted an unsolicited bid for an M4/M4A1 procurement contract. The FN bid was rejected, but Colt threatened a huge lawsuit against the DOD. In 1997, however, an agreement was reached by which

Colt would drop all claims for damages in return for the "M4 Addendum," which recognized Colt as the "sole source" provider for M4 procurement – an agreement that would continue until 2009. Undeterred, FN submitted a further unsolicited proposal to manufacture M4/M4A1s in May 1998, after the US Army announced a contract with Colt for the manufacture of 15,925 of the carbines. When FN's proposal was rejected, the company took its case to the US Court of Federal Claims, but lost.

Between the late 1990s and 2009, therefore, Colt was the sole provider of M4/M4A1s. This led to no small measure of controversy, especially as the prices of the M4 and the M4A1 climbed sharply during the United States' subsequent Global War on Terrorism (GWOT). In December 1999, the price of an M4 was $521; by December 2010, the price of an individual carbine had risen to $1,221 (Watters 2011). During this period both the escalating price and questions raised concerning the M4/M4A1's reliability (which some viewed as politically motivated to undermine the "sole source" provision) resulted in the weapon experiencing a turbulent time in terms of its profile. What it did not stop, however, was the exponential growth in the popularity of the weapon and a great surge in acquisition (see the Use chapter).

US troops lay down their M4 carbines during an inventory exercise. All the weapons are fitted with the AN/PEQ-15 ATPIAL device on the forward rails. The dual lenses on the ATPIAL are the infrared aim laser and the visible aim laser, while the single lens is the infrared illuminator. (TONY KARUMBA/AFP/Getty Images)

THE M4A1 AND WEAPON IMPROVEMENTS

The M4 carbine was designed primarily for use by auxiliary troops, weapon support teams, and vehicle crews. Given the historical adoption of CAR-15 weapons by US SOF, however, it was natural that the American special-forces community would take an interest in the weapon. The M4A1 was initially produced with this group squarely in mind. At first, almost the only difference between the M4 and the M4A1 was that the latter weapon replaced the three-round burst with a full-auto setting, reflecting SOF troops' preference for full-auto fire in close-quarters battle (CQB) actions. During operations in Afghanistan and Iraq, however, it became apparent that the barrel fitted to the M4A1 was not well suited to the prodigious ammunition consumption of front-line SOCOM operators, some barrels failing under heavy sustained-fire use (see the Use chapter for a fuller analysis). To solve the problem, Colt developed a heavier barrel for SOCOM operators, the barrel having a substantially increased diameter in the section between the receiver and the front sight block. Although Colt itself designated the heavy-barrel M4A1 as the Model 921HB, as opposed to the standard-barrel Model 921, both weapons are still referred to as the M4A1 carbine in US military terminology.

The fitting of the heavy barrel is just one of a plethora of incremental improvements the M4/M4A1 has undergone since the early 1990s, with more than 90 such modifications. These have included internal changes such as an improved bolt-carrier group, new ejector spring, and new gas ring; and in 2010 the M4A1 acquired an ambidextrous fire-control assembly, enabling the operator to move the selector lever from one side of the weapon to the other. There have also been extensive modifications based on external fittings and accessories, such as rails, optics, laser designators, bipods, and slings.

A key phase in the M4/M4A1's evolution has been the Product Improvement Program (PIP), which began in 2011 alongside the Individual Carbine competition. There have been two phases to the PIP. Phase I is the fleet conversion of M4s to M4A1 standard, with an authorized upgrade of 300,000 M4s including the heavier barrel, full-auto capability, and ambidextrous fire controls. Phase II of the PIP focused on "future improvements for the M4A1 Carbine to deliver enhanced reliability, durability, ergonomics and zero retention" (PEO Soldier 2012). A core focus of this phase was to seek improvements in the weapon's fundamental operating mechanism, specifically the bolt and bolt-carrier assembly. Between 2012 and 2013, six months of evaluation and testing were conducted on 11 competing designs, but the eventual conclusion was that none of the alternatives outperformed the existing components, so the competition was brought to an early close. Improvements in forward rail design were continued, however, feeding into the adoption of the Rail Adapter System (RAS) made by Knight's Armament Corporation (KAC), which subsequently became an integral part of the M4 Modular Weapon System (MWS).

The Individual Carbine competition was an open proposal to replace the M4A1 with an entirely different weapon. Six companies, or groups of companies, ultimately submitted proposals: FN Herstal of Belgium; Heckler & Koch of Germany; Beretta of Italy; Colt; Adcor Defense; and a joint proposal from Remington, Magpul, and Bushmaster. In 2013,

however, the US Army announced the suspension of the competition. Several reasons underpinned the Army's decision, including the fact that the M4A1 was a pretty good weapon to start with, but also that the test weapons used the new high-pressure M855A1 Enhanced Performance Round 5.56×45mm cartridge, which caused reliability issues for all the weapons involved. In June 2013, therefore, the Army extended the suspension by announcing that "the Individual Carbine (IC) competition will formally conclude without the selection of a winner. None of the carbines evaluated during the testing phase of the competition met the minimum scoring requirement needed to continue to the next phase of the evaluation" (US Army 2013). Colt's submission for the competition, incidentally, was the CM901 (Colt Modular 901), immediately recognizable as being derived from the M16/M4 series, with the same core AR-15 operating mechanism and controls. One of the CM901's key differences, however, was that the upper receiver and barrel could be swapped for other units to change the caliber of the carbine: options were 5.56×45mm NATO, 6.8×43mm Remington SPC, 7.62×39mm, and 7.62×51mm NATO. The lower receiver had an enlarged magazine well that took the various sizes of magazine. The upper receiver also had its own individual rail system.

The modern M4A1 is the product of a long evolution, albeit an evolution that occurred more quickly in the hothouse of war. Following the end of Colt's "sole source" contract, Remington won a contract for a production run of 120,000 M4A1s, and dramatically undercut the price of each weapon for the US Army, dropping it to $673 per carbine. Colt, whose agreement with the DOD still required future manufacturers to pay a royalty on each M4/M4A1 supplied to the US military, contested the decision to award the contract to Remington, setting in motion a round of political infighting. The outcome of was that the DOD had to solicit

An Australian Army soldier prepares to fire his M4 carbine, heavily accessorized with an ACOG optic, M203 underbarrel grenade launcher, and an electronic targeting system. Many M4s, when upgraded to M4A1 standard, have received ambidextrous selector levers. (Cpl James Gulliver/Public domain photograph from defenseimagery.mil)

THE M4 CARBINE EXPOSED

5.56×45mm M4A1 CQBR

This cutaway shows the major internal working parts of an M4A1 fitted with a Close Quarter Battle Receiver (CQBR). A cartridge has just been fired: the hammer has been released, driving the firing pin forward into the primer of the cartridge case, which is shown positioned in the chamber. The bullet travels down the barrel. Once the bullet passes the gas port, set beneath the rear section of the front sight mount, a proportion of gas is diverted down the gas tube and vented into the upper receiver. The M4/M4A1, as with all AR-15-style firearms, is a direct-impingement firearm, meaning that the gas ported off from the barrel is channeled directly onto the bolt carrier, driving the bolt carrier and bolt rearward through the cartridge extraction and ejection processes (this contrasts with piston-operated gas mechanisms that have a piston arrangement separating the gas from the bolt carrier). The bolt carrier travels back, re-cocking the hammer and trigger and compressing the recoil spring; at its fullest extent of travel it is arrested by the buffer, then begins its forward travel again under the released energy of the recoil spring. On this return journey, the bolt strips a new cartridge from the magazine and chambers it, and the eight-lug bolt is rotated to the right via a lug-and-cam arrangement to lock into the barrel extension for safe firing.

1. Detachable buttstock	**12.** Barrel	**23.** Gas tube
2. Buffer assembly	**13.** Magazine	**24.** Bolt assembly
3. Upper receiver	**14.** Trigger	**25.** Chamber
4. Back-up Iron Sight (BUIS)	**15.** Pistol grip	**26.** Ejection-port cover (open)
5. MIL-STD-1913 rail	**16.** Lower receiver	**27.** Magazine well
6. Rail Adapter System (RAS)	**17.** Stock adjuster	**28.** Magazine follower
7. Gas port	**18.** Sling swivel, rear	**29.** Magazine spring
8. Front sight	**19.** Charging handle assembly	**30.** Hammer spring
9. Stepped heavy barrel	**20.** Automatic sear hook	**31.** Disconnector
10. Flash suppressor	**21.** Hammer	**32.** Automatic sear
11. Sling swivel, front	**22.** Bolt carrier	**33.** Forward assist

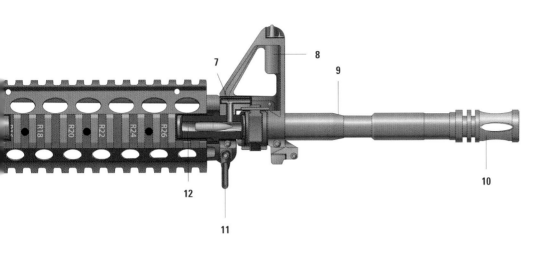

The adaptor block mechanism of the Colt LE901-16S, the semiautomatic variant of the Colt CM901. The block enables the weapon to use magazines of different calibers, with a corresponding change in the barrel and the upper receiver. (FilmWerks/ Wikimedia/ CC BY-SA 3.0)

new bids from the vendors, and this time FN Herstal won the contract. FN's winning of subsequent large contracts – one in 2020 was worth $119 million – means that the Belgian company is at the forefront of the M4/M4A1's future. Remington does, however, also manufacture M4A1-type weapons for the international civilian, law-enforcement, and military markets. Its R4, for example, is essentially an M4A1 and is fully compatible with standard M4/M4A1 parts; it is used by the Philippine Army and Marine Corps, and at the time of writing is also under contract for Foreign Military Sales to the US Army.

MODULARITY

The M4/M4A1's development story is only partly the story of the weapon itself. The other part comes from the optimization of the weapon's potential through the very extensive range of tactical accessories that can be fitted to its rail systems.

The driving force behind M4 accessorization has been the Special Operations Peculiar Modification (SOPMOD) kit program established in 1992 at NSWC-Crane. Prior to this program, the US SOF community had recognized the need for tactical accessories that could increase target recognition/acquisition, speed of engagement, accuracy, and comfort of weapons handling, in both day and night conditions. Early attempts to fulfill this requirement for the CAR-15 weapons were thoroughly improvisational, with off-the-shelf optical sights, pointers, lights, grenade launchers, and other contraptions added via clamps, tape, and other DIY adaptations. The foundations of a more professional and consistent approach were laid with the Special Operations Special Technology (SOST) Modular Close Combat Carbine Project of 1989. SOST took the

Block 1

SOPMOD M4 Accessory Kit

Special Operations Peculiar Modification to the M4 Carbine

Poster Version 3 February 2005

Block I Accessory Kit

Logistics Support: sofsustainment@navy.mil
Website: http://ssavie.socom.mil

Reflex Sight
NSN: 1240-01-435-1916

ECOS-N
NSN: 1240-01-495-1385

AN/PEQ-5 Carbine
Visible Laser
NSN: 5860-01-439-5409

AN/PVS-17A Mini Night Vision Sight
NSN: 5855-01-474-8904

4X Day Optical Scope
NSN: 1240-01-412-6608

AN/PEQ-2 Infrared Illuminator
NSN: 5855-01-422-5253

Backup Iron Sight
NSN: 1005-01-449-6306

Visible Bright Light II
NSN: 5855-01-501-3081

Universal Pocketscope
Mount (PVS14)
NSN: 5855-01-482-6164

(PVS18) NSN: 5855-01-485-7749
(M68) NSN: 5855-01-485-7755

M4A1 Carbine w/Carrying Handle
NSN: 1005-01-382-0953

Forward Handgrip
NSN: 1005-01-416-1091

Sound Suppressor Kit
NSN: 1005-01-437-0324

Rail Interface System
NSN: 1005-01-416-1089

Grenade Launcher Mount
NSN: 1055-01-416-1090

M203 9" Barrel Assembly
NSN: 1010-01-410-7422

Grenade Launcher
Leaf Sight
NSN: 1010-01-418-4588

AN/PSQ-18A
M203 Day/Night Sight
NSN: 1010-01-516-0953

emerging M4 carbine prototype and fitted it with various accessories, illustrating how from the outset the M4 was envisaged as the heart of a weapon system, and not purely a standalone weapon. The SOST program was further refined in the SOPMOD program, although slow procurement and a hesitant buy-in from other component commands meant that the SOPMOD program did not really become a meaningful reality until the late 1990s.

SOPMOD Block I transformed the M4A1. Its extensive "shopping list" of accessories meant that the SOCOM operator could tailor his weapon precisely to the required mission, from ultra-close-range high-value target missions in darkened buildings through to medium-range open-country engagements requiring accurate distance shooting. The Block I equipment consisted of the following items: 4× day optical scope (Trijicon TA01NSN 4×32mm Advanced Combat Optical Gunsight – ACOG); reflex sight (Trijicon Model RX01M4A1); ECOS-N optical sight (red-dot-type reflex sight, a variant of the Aimpoint CompM2); rail interface system (MIL-STD-1913); vertical forward handgrip; quick-attach/-detach M203 grenade launcher mount and sight; M203 40mm barrel assembly; sound suppressor kit (KAC quick-detach sound suppressor – QDSS); AN/PEQ-2 infrared illuminator (Insight Technology); AN/PEQ-5 carbine visible laser (Insight Technology); AN/PVS-17A mini night-vision sight (Insight Technology); AN/PSQ-18A M203 day/night sight (Insight Technology); visible bright light (Insight Technology Visible

This official SOPMOD poster shows the range of tactical accessories available in the Block I kit. The kit provides the operator with the ability to fight in both day and night conditions, in combat situations from close-quarters battle (CQB) to almost Designated Marksman (DM) ranges. (USSOCOM/Wikimedia/Public Domain)

Lance Corporal Ryan Pettis, a team leader with Scout Sniper Platoon, 1st Battalion, 7th Marine Regiment, has an M4A1 fitted with a Knight's Armament NT4 QDSS suppressor. (Photo by Cpl. Joseph Scanlan, 1st Marine Division, USMC)

Light Illuminator – VLI); universal pocket scope mount; combat sling; and a sloping cheek weld buttstock (referred to as the "Crane Stock").

Since it was issued, the SOPMOD kit program has been through several more stages and blocks of revision, adding, subtracting, and improving the equipment spectrum. (A more detailed treatment of SOPMOD accessories in particular can be found in McNab 2019: 56–65.) Tactical accessorization has not just been the preserve of the US SOF community, however. With the addition of the RAS, in addition to the Rail Interface System (RIS), both the M16 and the M4/M4A1 carbines have become the core of the Modular Weapon System (MWS), essentially a pared-down version of the SOPMOD accessories range that provides the regular infantryman with his own toolkit of tactical options.

As defined in the US Army's *Rifle and Carbine* manual in 2016, for example, the MWS has four main sight offerings. First, the standard aperture iron sights are built into the weapon's carrying handle, adjustable for both azimuth (wind) and elevation and generally good for shooting out to 300m (328yd). Second, as most M4/M4A1s are issued or used without the carrying handle, the BUIS provides an iron-sight option for fitting to the top rail. It is a flip-up aperture sight that provides a backup capability effective technically out to 600m (656yd), although the limitations of human vision make engagement at this range with only iron sights a challenging feat. Third, the M68 Close Combat Optic (CCO), the

US military designation for the Aimpoint CompM2, is a red-dot reflex-type sight ideal for fast target acquisition and shooting at ranges of less than 200m (219yd). Finally, the M150 Rifle Combat Optic (RCO), the US military designation for the highly popular Trijicon ACOG, is available in various different models, from 1.5× to 6× magnification, and, through the reticle's bullet-drop compensator, enables the soldier to take aimed shots out to 600m (656yd).

In addition to the standard optical sights, the MWS includes a range of thermal weapon sight (TWS) options from Raytheon's AN/PAS-13 series which, as the manual explains, use "forward-looking infrared technology that identify the infrared emitted radiation (heat) of a field of view, and translate those temperatures into a gray- or color-scaled image" (US Army 2016: 59). The MWS also includes a selection of pointer/illuminator/aiming lights, which are usually clamped either on top of or to the side of the RAS. As listed in the 2016 manual, these are: the AN/PEQ-2 (Infrared Target Pointer/Illuminator/Aiming Light, or ITPIAL); the AN/PEQ-15 (Advanced Target Pointer/Illuminator/Aiming Light, or ATPIAL); the AN/PEQ-15A (Dual Beam Aiming Laser – Advanced2, or DBAL-A2); and the AN/PSQ-23 (Illuminator, Integrated, Small Arms, also known as the Small Tactical Optical Rifle Mounted (STORM) Micro Laser Rangefinder (MLRF)). Each confers different advantages, but all project visible and infrared light to illuminate the target and guide accurate shooting.

When the soldier is wearing night-vision goggles (NVGs) while using the TWS, he can see infrared-light projections that are completely invisible to an enemy with no night-vision capability. This technological advantage has provided US troops with a leading tactical advantage during nighttime or low-light engagements. In some actions, American fireteams or larger units have designated their targets almost at leisure before opening fire simultaneously; the enemy personnel were completely unaware that they were being "painted" until they were shot. Visible-light attachments are

An M4 carbine with SOPMOD accessories and treated from muzzle to stock in full camo paint. Such treatments need to ensure that the external paint does not interfere with moving parts such as triggers, selector levers, and ejection port covers. (Verunka96/Wikimedia/CC BY-SA 3.0)

This US Marine in Afghanistan in 2010 is armed with the Mk 12 Mod 0/1 SPR, a Designated Marksman rifle based on the AR-15 platform. Although it fires the same cartridge as the M4/M4A1, it has an effective range of 700m (766yd). (Lance Cpl. Jorge A. Ortiz, US Marine Corps/Wikimedia/Public Domain)

also very useful for boresighting weapons. Many US Army soldiers and US Marines also use one of the many weapon-mounted lights on their

Trijicon and Specter reticles (opposite)

The Trijicon ACOG close-combat optic (**1**) is one of the defining sights for the M4/M4A1, having been designed specifically for these weapons. It is a fixed-power scope with magnification levels from 1.5× to 6× (here we see the 4×32 scope) and a battery-free illuminated reticle – the optic is charged by natural light. The key element of the ACOG reticle is the central bullet-drop compensator; the application of this reticle is demonstrated on page 28.

The Specter OS4× Optical Sight (**2**) is a fixed-power 4× optical telescopic weapon sight with a 32mm (1.25in) objective lens. The reticle has two "modes": a central aiming feature (the cross at the center of the crosshairs) and a range-estimating and drop compensation reticle. A reticle illumination knob on the top of the sight (the sight is battery powered) enables the operator to adjust the relative brightness of the two reticle modes.

The Specter DR (**3**) is a fast-switching dual 1× and 4× fixed optical power telescopic sight. Unlike the Specter OS4× it has an integrated peep-type BUIS mounted on the top rear of the main sight housing. The flick of a lever on the side of the sight provides the option for switching between power modes, the 1× setting for CQB and the 4× setting for longer-range engagements.

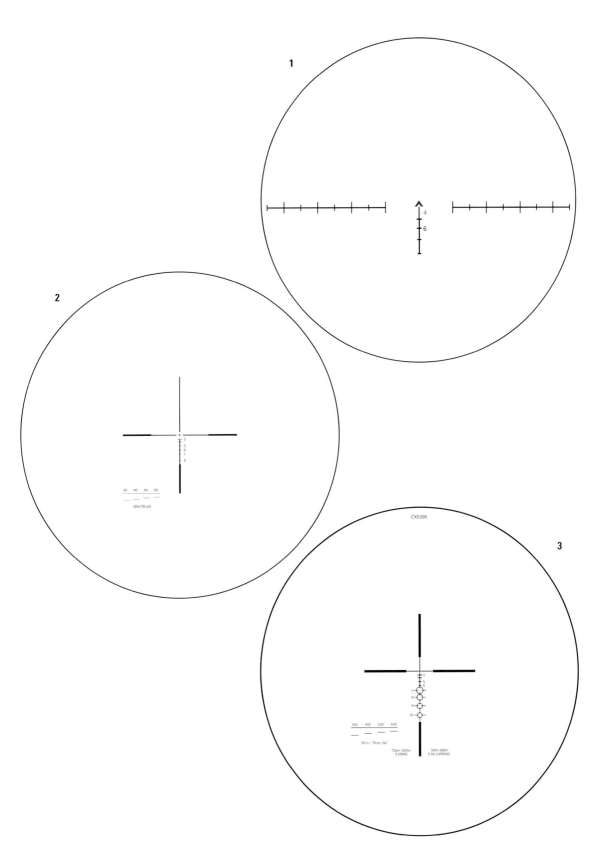

25

Chief Mass Communication Specialist Paula Ludwick, US Navy, shoots at a target during a Navy Rifle Qualification Course. Her M4A1 has a CQBR with a 10.3in barrel and a shortened RAS. Note the modern Magpul PMAG Gen M3 30-round window polymer magazine. (US Navy photo by Mass Communication Specialist 1st Class James Foehl/Released/ Wikimedia/Public Domain)

M4/M4A1s. These are essentially gun-mounted flashlights; the more sophisticated varieties can be adjusted between white-light and infrared-light projection.

Beyond sighting options, the MWS includes more kinetic attachments. The M320/M320A1 and M203 are both 40mm underbarrel grenade launchers, capable of firing illumination, smoke, signal, high-explosive (HE), high-explosive, dual purpose (HEDP – suited for use against personnel and light vehicles), non-lethal, and training practice rounds.

Aimpoint, EOTech, and Meprolight reticles (opposite)

The Aimpoint CompM3 (**1**) is a red-dot sight, designed to be used by an operator who has both eyes open for maximum awareness of target and surroundings. The red dot follows the user's eye motion but remains fixed on the target. The sight is available in two dot sizes (2 and 4 minutes of angle) and is compatible for night-vision devices (NVDs).

The EOTech Holographic Weapon Sight (HWT; **2**) is a non-magnifying sight that projects a holographic reticle into the viewer's field of vision. Like the red-dot-type sights, the HWT optimizes the user's peripheral awareness, and allows for shooting with both eyes open. The reticle brightness can be adjusted according to the external light levels.

Developed in Israel, the Meprolight Mepro M21 (**3**) is a red-dot sight, self-illuminated by a fiber-optic collector system during the day and by tritium at night; it can also be paired with NVGs. It has a 1× magnification, and is specifically designed for CQB.

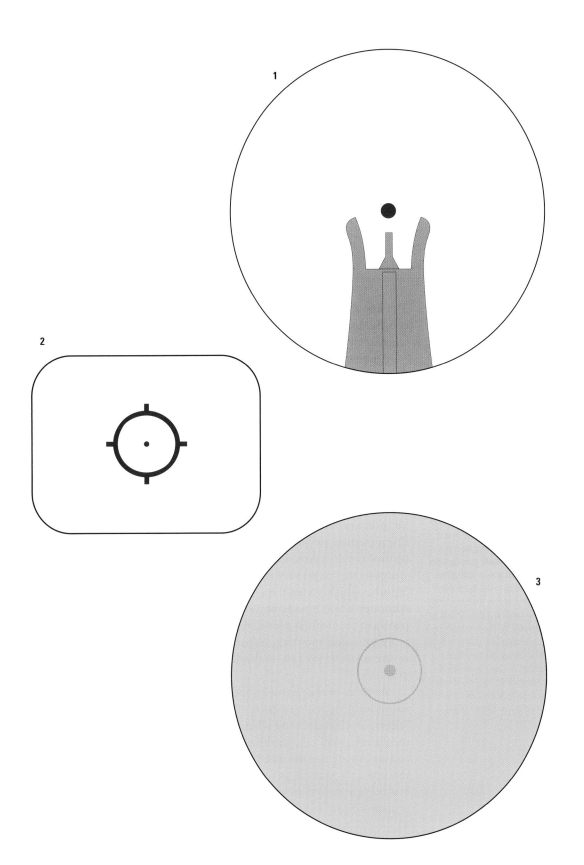

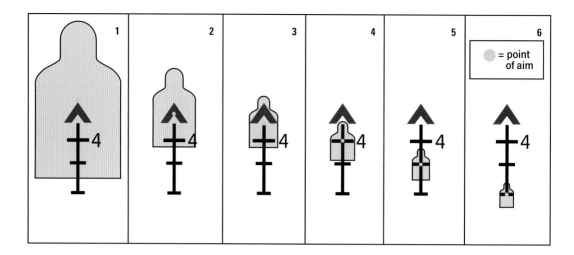

The ACOG's bullet-drop compensator enables the operator to adjust the aim point according to the parabolic drop of the bullet over various ranges. The base of the inverted V-shaped reticle and the stadia lines below represent the average width of a man's shoulders (482mm/19in) at the ranges indicated. The operator can use the reticle both to estimate range and to put the 5.56mm rounds on target at up to 600m (656yd). For example, in (**1**) if the red chevron is no wider than the target's head, then the target is at 100m range or less. If the chevron is wider than the head but narrower than the body (**2**), this indicates a 100–200m (109–219yd) range, but if the chevron matches the body width (**3**) the range is 300m (328yd). At 400m (437yd), the first hash mark is the same width as the body (**4**), and if the second hash mark matches the body width (**5**) this indicates 500m (547yd). Finally, the third hash mark (**6**) shows the body width at 600m (656yd).

The key difference between the two systems is that the M320/M320A1 can be dismounted from the M4 and used as a standalone weapon, whereas the M203 can only be used when mounted on the weapon.

Another interesting underbarrel attachment is the M26 Modular Accessory Shotgun System (MASS), a compact 12-gauge shotgun feeding from a three- or five-round detachable box magazine. It can fire slug rounds for door breaching, 00 buckshot for short-range antipersonnel use, and the full spectrum of shotgun shell types, including non-lethal types.

To improve ergonomics and handling, optional vertical foregrips are common MWS fittings on the M4/M4A1 carbine (and on the standard M16 rifle). Foregrips have a range of benefits for the soldier, such as muscle relief for the front arm by offering different grip options; but the primary tactical benefit lies in recoil control, especially when fast firing (similar to how the front grip on a hammer drill helps the user control the drill direction), and the ability to swing the front end of the weapon onto target very rapidly. Some vertical grips come with integral bipods, which extend on legs out of the bottom of the foregrip. Although these bipods do not provide the stable or finely adjustable platform of a regular bipod, they do give an immediate foundation for more precision shooting. Adjustable external bipods can also be fitted to the lower front rail; multiple commercial and military models are available.

While tactical accessories undoubtedly enable the M4/M4A1 carbine to perform at its very best, the user has to exercise discretion and judgment when deciding what to fit. Adding too many accessories can turn a relatively light carbine into a very heavy system, which in turn can actually retard the speed of tactical shooting. The general rule is that the operator should only fit accessories that significantly contribute toward the mission or to survivability. Familiarity with the accessories is also critical: a soldier who is an expert with iron sights is far more dangerous than a soldier who has all the kit, but who is inexperienced in its use.

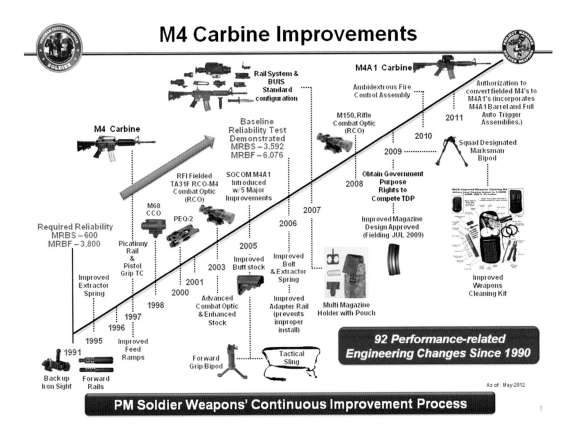

M4 Carbine Improvements

92 Performance-related Engineering Changes Since 1990

As of: May-2012

PM Soldier Weapons' Continuous Improvement Process

1

One particularly interesting line of development with the SOPMOD Block II program was the offering of two alternative upper receivers: the Special Purpose Receiver (SPR) and the Close Quarter Battle Receiver (CQBR). The SPR used a new upper receiver for an 18in threaded-muzzle match-grade free-floating stainless-steel heavy barrel; accompanied by an integral front bipod and appropriate optics, the M4A1 in this configuration was now a semiautomatic Designated Marksman rifle. It was subsequently type-classified by the US Navy as the Mk 12 Mod 0/1 SPR, the "SPR" now standing for "Special Purpose Rifle," to indicate that it was now a standalone weapon, and not just a SOPMOD upper receiver.

The CQBR took the opposite route. Its replacement upper receiver was for a reduced-length barrel of just 10.3in, taking the weapon down to the dimensions of the Colt Commando. The weapon has, like the Mk 12 Mod 0/1 SPR, received its own independent type classification: Mk 18 Mod 0, or the Mk 18 Mod 1 with a sightless gas block and full-length accessory rail kit.

A compact description of the evolution of the M4/M4A1 necessarily has to take several shortcuts. In this study, for example, the focus has principally been on the main lines of development with the US manufacturers and for the US military. The M4/M4A1 has, however, been the subject of huge global distribution to law-enforcement personnel and civilian shooters. The M4/M4A1, or variant thereof, is just as likely to be found in the back of a police car in many countries as on the battlefield.

This presentation slide from the Program Executive Office Soldier (PEO Soldier) provides a visual overview of some of the temporal landmarks in the development of the M4/M4A1 carbine. The abbreviation "MRBS" stands for Mean Rounds Between Stoppage, while "MRBF" indicates Mean Rounds Between Failure. (US Army/Program Executive Office Soldier (PEO Soldier)/ Wikimedia/Public Domain)

USE
Two decades of combat testing

The M150 RCO – the US military designation for the TA31RCO Variant of the ACOG optic – is one of the most common sight fittings on the M4/M4A1. It provides an improved capability to recognize and engage targets from 300m to 600m (328yd to 656yd). (Photo courtesy of PEO Soldier/ Wikimedia/Public Domain)

The basic handling characteristics of the M4 are largely those of any other weapon in the AR-15 family, including the M16 rifles. The key difference is principally in terms of ballistic performance. Before addressing that controversial discussion, however, and before we explore the M4's general use as a practical combat tool, we need some explanation of how the carbine is handled physically.

This overview is more than just a rote description of mechanical movements. During the roughly two decades in which the M4/M4A1 and similar compact carbines have risen to near dominance in Western armies, much else has changed in terms of the kit, equipment, training, and tactics of the infantryman. In addition, many armies have experienced the immersive and brutal combat laboratories of Afghanistan and Iraq. These factors have led to the sharp refinement of carbine handling techniques, not just within the SOF community but also more widely with infantry units. As the conflicts in Afghanistan and Iraq quickly taught, the key to winning a close-quarters firefight – the type of action for which the M4/M4A1 is best suited – is the combination of both accurate shooting *and* extremely fast handling. By "handling" I mean not only the essential actions of loading, reloading, and clearance drills, but also the ways of mounting the weapon when both static and moving, and how to aim the weapon during fast-moving encounters.

Underpinning this discussion is an important point. In its original conception, the M4 carbine was more of a rear-echelon firearm, or a weapon to be stored by vehicle crews as a last-ditch personal defense. It was not originally intended to be a mass-distribution front-line combat weapon, to be run hot and fast not only by regular infantry, but also by SOF personnel. It is crucial to bear this in mind, particularly in discussions of the M4's performative merits. It is also true, however, that the

capabilities of any weapon can be enhanced by smooth and confident handling. Judging by the sheer volume of YouTube topics dedicated precisely to this issue, the M4's handling has been extensively debated, tweaked, and adjusted, which with tactical accessorization (see below) has maximized the combat capability of the weapon.

US Navy Petty Officer 3rd Class Garrett Griffin fires an M4 carbine during a low-light weapons qualification course aboard the guided-missile destroyer USS *Carney* (DDG-64) in the Atlantic Ocean, May 20, 2019. (Mass Communication Specialist 1st Class Fred Gray IV/US Navy/ Wikimedia/Public Domain)

BASIC OPERATION AND ERGONOMIC ISSUES

The physical handling of the M4 carbine is, to a large degree, dictated by one of the key idiosyncrasies of its design – the location of the charging handle at the top and back of the upper receiver. This configuration makes the AR-15 family unique, and also pours fuel onto the flames of the argument between the M4's detractors and proponents. The overwhelming majority of selective-fire carbines and rifles have the charging handle located on the right or upper side of the receiver; others (particularly weapons manufactured by Heckler & Koch) position it on the forend. Having the charging handle in these locations, particularly on the right side of the receiver, is fairly intuitive. It allows the operator (assumed to be a right-handed male) to draw back the charging handle using the full power and range of the arm, either with his right hand or by reaching over with his left hand, which permits retention of pistol grip, although the weapon has to be canted over a little to the left to perform this action. The key advantage to the "conventional" location of the charging handle, however, is that the operator does not need to break cheek weld and even sight alignment to manipulate the handle. This is particularly advantageous

Specialist Chad Wagner of the 3d Battalion, 8th Cavalry Regiment, 3d Brigade Combat Team, 1st Cavalry Division, checks the chamber of an M4 carbine. The location of the charging handle arguably makes operating the M4 rather less intuitive than weapons with side-mounted charging handles. (Spc. Brandon Banzhaf/US Army/Wikimedia/Public Domain)

when clearing weapon malfunctions in active firefights, as the shooter can essentially keep his weapon squarely in the shoulder and trained in the direction of the enemy while clearing a stoppage (as long as the cause of that stoppage is not too complex). On the debit side, however, the shooter who makes a right-hand operation of drawing back the charging handle has to relinquish his hold on the pistol grip.

There is an inherent awkwardness in the operation of the M4's charging handle, even if that awkwardness is eventually overcome – and fluently so – by practice and familiarity. A right-handed shooter mounting the weapon in the right shoulder has to keep a grip on the forend with his left hand, pulling the weapon into the shoulder (to anchor the weapon) while canting it downward to give access to the T-handle. If cocking with the left hand (the more typical process), the stock is either retained in the right shoulder or trapped between the right arm and the torso, and is pointed either up or down to allow for cocking. What cannot be done in either case is to retain cheek weld on the stock: the head has to be lifted up and out of sight alignment. One advantage that the M4/M4A1 has in this process over the standard M16 rifles is that it has less weight out front by virtue of having a shorter barrel, which means that the operator has more of the weapon's weight over his center of gravity when performing the process.

The configuration of the M4/M4A1 raises a central question: Why opt for this type of layout at all? Two chief reasons appear to have inspired Eugen Stoner's location of the AR-15 charging handle. First, it eliminates the protrusion of a side-mounted charging handle, which could get caught on foliage, straps, and horizontal surfaces. Second, the AR-15's

configuration means that the operator can maintain his hold on the pistol grip while performing a weapon clearance, although any credited advantages here are somewhat undone by the requirement for the operator to lift his head off the stock to make re-cocking possible.

As with many aspects of the AR-15 series, the location of the charging handle has led to lively debate. If anything, the balance of opinion seems to be toward the weapon's detractors. The very fact that almost all other assault rifles and carbines – some of them very fine pieces of kit at that – opt for the side-mounted charging handle speaks volumes, and more than mere convention.

Before coming fully down on the side of the detractors, however, the general satisfaction felt by hundreds of thousands of troops toward the

M4/M4A1, including large numbers among the highly demanding SOF community, indicates that the location of the charging handle is not a genuine practical problem, as long as training makes operation of the system second nature. Indeed, the AR-15 platform is so familiar to so many military personnel that many weapon designers have used it as the basis of advanced new weapons. The HK 416 and HK 417 are cases in point.

LOADING AND FIRING

The basic operating sequence of the M4 carbine, based on a weapon that has been proven clear and with no magazine inserted, is as follows:

First, the selector lever is placed on "Safe." The bolt is opened and locked into place by pulling the charging handle back to its fullest extent and pressing the lower portion of the bolt-release button. With this action, the bolt is held back and the ejection port is also opened, so the operator can inspect the chamber to ensure that it is clear. Note that when the bolt is locked back, the charging handle remains at the rear of its travel. There is no independent charging handle spring to return the handle to its starting position, so the user must slide it forward manually. It is important to do this as the charging handle piece is very light, and if damaged would render the weapon inoperable until replaced.

Second, with the bolt locked open, the operator inserts a loaded magazine into the magazine well, pushing it up until it makes a positive click engagement with the magazine-release catch. It is regarded as good practice to pull down on the magazine after insertion to ensure that it is seated properly, as there is typically enough tension in the magazine-release catch to retain a magazine without it being fully seated.

Third, with the magazine in place, the operator presses the upper, larger part of the bolt-release catch. This releases the bolt, which runs forward, strips the first round off the top of the magazine, and chambers it. The swelling at the top of the bolt-release catch is positioned so that it can be disengaged with a quick palm slap – appreciated by troops rushing to get back into action during an intense firefight.

Fourth, the operator now shoulders the weapon ready to fire. Using his thumb, he pushes the selector lever around to either semi-auto or three-round burst (M4)/full-auto (M4A1) and begins engaging the target.

When the magazine is empty, the bolt automatically locks to the rear, which facilitates a quick magazine change: the empty magazine is ejected, a new one is inserted, and the bolt-release button is slapped again to send the bolt forward, strip the first round off the top of the new magazine, and chamber it. Note that if the bolt is in the closed position on an empty chamber, the process of chambering a new round requires nothing more than pulling the charging handle back and releasing it; the charging handle is carried back to its forward position with the bolt carrier.

The procedure for loading and firing the M4/M4A1 carbine is, therefore, a reasonably straightforward one, and apart from some differences in ergonomics relating to the placement of the charging handle,

the weapon works on largely the same core principles as most other assault rifles and carbines.

FORWARD ASSIST

One element that benefits from further comment, however, is the forward assist mechanism, which is the thumb-operated device located on the right side of the receiver, designed to ensure that the bolt is fully in battery before firing. The forward assist is something of a debatable feature, however. It was introduced in the early and problematic years of the M16 rifle's evolution, as a mechanical means of dealing with poor chambering due to excessive fouling. In reality, the reliability problems of the M16 were more to do with propellant type than the M16's design, and once the chamber and bore were chrome lined and the ammunition improved (changes embodied in the M16A1) any need for the forward assist decreased significantly. (For more about the early problems of the M16, see Rottman 2011.) Arguably, the forward assist became something of a redundancy, there more for psychological reassurance than practical reliance.

While the forward assist might now seem to lack technical necessity for someone who does not take weapons into the brutal school of combat, opinions are less sharply divided within the military community. A useful, if somewhat informal, insight into the arguments for and against the forward assist is set out in an article by firearms expert Keith Wood

26th Marine Expeditionary Unit Maritime Raid Force Marines fire M4 carbines while participating in a marksmanship training exercise at a range in Qatar, April 22, 2013. The squatting posture, walking from the knees rather than the hips, reduces weapon movement while on the move. (US Marine Corps photo by Cpl. Christopher Q. Stone/Released/Wikimedia/ Public Domain)

Israeli soldiers of the IDF's Alpine Unit, armed with M4 carbines, conduct winter warfare training on Mount Hermon. For subzero operations, the M4/M4A1 requires appropriate forms of lubrication and furniture that does not become brittle in the cold. (Israel Defense Forces/ Wikimedia/Public Domain)

(2013). Wood has a certain ambivalence toward the feature, seeing it as something of an anachronism given the subsequent improvements to the AR-15 platform – he notes that some modern US weapons based on the AR-15 platform, such as the 7.62×51mm SR25/M110, have dispensed with the forward assist altogether – but also appreciating the sense of security that it provides. He also acknowledges the feature's backup practicality, in that it is not uncommon for firearms to need a little assistance into battery. He adds the point that in a hunting scenario, it is sometimes important to be able to close the bolt quietly by riding the charging handle slowly forward; the forward assist ensures that at the end of this process the cartridge is properly seated. Although official M4/M4A1 carbine manual advice explains that this action is not advised, one can see why SOF operators might need to do so during covert operations, and having the forward assist provides reassurance that the weapon is ready to go.

For front-line judgments, however, Wood turns to five highly experienced former military operators: Kyle Lamb, Larry Vickers, Rick Shuck, and James Jarrett, all former US Army SOF, and firearms designer Chris Barrett. The balance of opinion from these experts is in favor of the forward assist. Interestingly, many of the operators say that they have never actually had to use the device, but in hot, dusty, and muddy environments, and in firefights where the operator is running multiple magazines through an increasingly dirty weapon, having the forward assist is potentially a life-saver. The main critic among the group, James Jarrett, points out that if the operator does not have confidence that the bolt will seat properly without application of the forward assist, then he probably should not have confidence that the weapon will seat properly during its normal cycle of operations. Jarrett acknowledges, however, that it doesn't hurt to have the feature. In general, therefore, we can probably best say that while the rationale for the forward assist is questionable, removing the feature altogether adds no benefit and potentially deletes a critical fallback, however rarely it may be used.

FIRE CONTROL AND NOISE

The M4 is a fairly accurate weapon. A study conducted by the Army Marksmanship Unit, comparing the accuracy of M4 carbines and M16 rifles straight from the rack with iron sights, found that while the full-length M16 rifle could fire a 24in group at 274m (300yd), the M4 carbine achieved a 32in group. The disparity between the two seems weighted significantly in favor of the M16, but given the basic iron sights and the M4's short barrel length, the results for the latter weapon are still respectable. Note that much of the accuracy equation is accounted for by the ammunition used: when match-grade ammunition was fired, the groups tightened up considerably for both the M16 and the M4, to 12in and 18in respectively; and given that the average male torso is about 18–19in wide, this indicates that the M4/M4A1 can be consistently on target at 300yd. We should also add that most M4/M4A1s today are equipped with advanced optics, which by improving target acquisition,

Fire Controlman Seaman Rachel Hubley fires a full-auto burst from an M4 carbine from the fantail of the guided-missile cruiser USS *Vella Gulf* (CG-72), July 2008. Note the installation of both the BUIS and the M68 CCO on the same top rail. (US Navy photo by Mass Communication Specialist Seaman Chad R. Erdmann/ Wikimedia/Public Domain)

observed shot impacts, range calculation, and drop/windage adjustment significantly improve the accuracy of the weapon system.

Depending on the variant and/or upgrade, the M4/M4A1 offers either three-round burst or full-auto fire. The three-round-burst function in the M16A2 and the M4 was initially seen as a way to improve efficiency in ammunition consumption – three rounds, delivered in a single trigger pull, was deemed sufficient to neutralize an opponent, but without a wasteful and prolonged burst of full-auto fire. Gradually, however, the M4A1 replaced the three-round-burst function with full-auto. Why? The first reason was a problem at the heart of the three-round-burst firing mechanism, hinted at, albeit slightly defensively, in this extract from the US Army's *Rifle Marksmanship M16A1, M16A2/3, M16A4, and M4 Carbine*:

> c. Burst Fire Mode (M16A2/A4 Rifle, M4 Carbine). When the selector lever is set on the BURST position (Figure 4-12), the rifle fires a three-round burst if the trigger is held to the rear during the complete cycle. The weapon continues to fire three-round bursts with each separate trigger pull as long as ammunition is in the magazine. Releasing the trigger or exhausting ammunition at any point in the three-round cycle interrupts fire, producing one or two shots. Reapplying the trigger only completes the interrupted cycle; it does not begin a new one. This is not a malfunction. The M16A2/4 and M4 disconnectors have a three-cam mechanism that continuously rotates with each firing cycle. Based on the position of the disconnector cam, the first trigger pull (after initial selection of the BURST position) can produce one, two, or three firing cycles before the trigger must be pulled again. The burst cam rotates until it reaches the stop notch. (US Army 2003: 4-9)

While some weapons on the market have three-round-burst resetters – meaning that the weapon resets to firing a full three-round burst even if fewer than three rounds were fired on the previous burst – the M4 carbine did not acquire such sophistication. The three-round burst therefore could produce an erratic pattern of shots, which meant that the operator could miss target opportunities that required a full three (or more than three) rounds. Full-auto fire means that the shooter can adjust his fire by trigger discipline alone. The potential for very wasteful use of ammunition can largely be corrected by proper training. In reality, however, on most occasions professional troops will opt for rapid aimed semi-auto fire rather than full-auto fire, the former giving the best blend of suppression and on-target rounds.

SUPPRESSORS

One increasingly prevalent trend is for troops, particularly SOF operators, in professional and reasonably funded armies to fit suppressors to their M4/M4A1s. A suppressor can be a useful addition to a combat weapon, helping to disguise the soldier's position through both noise and flash

reduction and bringing other benefits, such as controlling muzzle climb (and therefore improving accuracy). Noise in particular has always been a problem with modern firearms. Both the M4/M4A1 and the M16 have an impulse noise of approximately 160dB, significantly above the 140dB deemed as the point at which noise levels become a hearing hazard. A mass firefight, in which dozens of M4/M4A1s and other even louder weapons are being discharged, is therefore a serious risk to auditory health, resulting in partial or even full hearing loss (temporary or permanent) and debilitating conditions such as tinnitus. Excessive firing noise also imposes significant restrictions on battlefield communications – it becomes difficult to hear both shouted and radio communications – making command and control problematic. Another, more psychological, effect is that soldiers can sometimes believe that their fire is more effective than it actually is, translating the noise generated as the effect on the enemy.

Suppressors work to reduce the sound of the gunshots significantly, through the expansion of the muzzle blast into a series of volume-softening baffles within the suppressor device. The key word here is "reduce," not "silence." It is largely a popular myth that firearms can be rendered almost entirely silent, giving out little more than a light "phut." Such weapons do exist, but they tend to be rare and highly specialized, used only by a rare few within special forces or other covert agencies, and are typically used in conjunction with subsonic ammunition. An M4/M4A1 fitted with an Advanced Armament Corp. (AAC) suppressor – AAC is one of the most popular makers of suppressors for M4-series weapons – has a noise signature of approximately 130dB – still equivalent to the volume

US Army 1st Lieutenant Jared Tomberlin, left, alongside an interpreter, scans the Afghan countryside through the ACOG optic on his M4A1 during a reconnaissance mission. He has fitted a foregrip bipod, a device that can provide a usefully stable shooting platform in rocky terrain. (DoD photo by Staff Sgt. Adam Mancini, US Army/Wikimedia/ Public Domain)

of a jackhammer and only just below the hazardous level, and well above if presented as a continuous noise in a firefight – but even this saving of approximately 30dB can be worth it. In 2016 it was announced that an entire battalion of troops within the 2d Marine Division would be equipped with suppressors on their M4s as a mass trial. Feedback from the trial suggested definite benefits, especially to command-and-control but also to the shooting performance of the troops; it was perceived that with quieter weapons, troops appeared to take a little more care with shot placement. Of course, there are downsides to using suppressors, most notably the addition of a significant forward weight to the M4/M4A1s's muzzle. The SureFire SOCOM 556, used by many US SOF units, adds 1.06lb to the weapon, making it heavier to swing and adding an extra muscular burden to the operator's front arm. Suppressors also get extremely hot during firing and under heavy use can wear out quickly, imposing an additional logistical burden on the forces. As is often the case with M4/M4A1 accessories, there are advantages and drawbacks to be considered.

TACTICAL HANDLING CHARACTERISTICS

The design rationale behind the M4 carbine was portability, and this quality was indeed central to its increasing adoption throughout the US military and by many other countries. Following the end of the Cold War, levels of mechanization and mobility have if anything increased further in professional armies. The M4/M4A1 has capitalized on this shift. With its stock retracted, the M4 measures just 29.75in, compared to a length of 39.5in for the fixed-stock versions of the M16. This genuinely significant reduction in storage length means the M4/M4A1 is an ideal weapon for handling in vehicles and helicopters, making it far more convenient to keep the weapon at the ready and also for bringing it up quickly to fire through open doors, windows, and firing ports.

An example of the value of the M4/M4A1 is this regard is evident in an extensive after-action report issued by the 3d Infantry Division (Mechanized) in July 2003 in the aftermath of Operation *Iraqi Freedom*. The report explains how the requirements for issuing weapons to the Marine Visitors Bureau (MVB) – a unit responsible for guarding VIPs moving through the division's Area of Operations (AO) – changed in response to vehicular deployment:

> Issue: Personal weapon MTOE [Modification Table of Organization and Equipment] change
> Discussion: After arriving in Kuwait, the MVB section found itself routinely escorting VIPs throughout high threat environments. This included picking up VIPs at Kuwait City International Airport among throngs of civilians and in vulnerable locations. During convoy operations for VIP escort missions, escort personnel were required to carry personal weapons inside the vehicles in the VIP convoy. Moreover, in accordance with policy, personnel were required to

A US Marine studies the landscape intently through his ACOG optic, atop his M4 carbine. This ACOG model has the BUIS on the top, in case the optics are damaged in action. (Marine Corps photo by Cpl. Darien J. Bjorndal/ Wikimedia/Public Domain)

maintain a locked, but not loaded status in the event of hostile fire. The personal weapon assigned to MVB personnel was the M-16A2, which is wholly unsuited for operation in a confined space such as a moving vehicle due to its size and length.

Recommendation: Protocol/MVB personnel should be required, by MTOE, to carry the M4 carbine or 9mm pistol as a personal weapon. The M4 carbine is similar to the M-16A2 in volume and rate of fire, but has a more compact size allowing for easier operation by VIP escorts under confined conditions. This recommendation is vital for ensuring the effective security of VIPs. (3d Infantry Division (Mechanized) 2003: 277)

The rationale behind the switch to the M4 for MVB personnel could not be clearer. The M4 offered the same firepower, but with easier handling characteristics in the confines of a vehicle, which had definite implications for the survivability of both the MVB team and the VIPs they were escorting. The M4 is short enough that an operator in a vehicle can rest the weapon's stock in his lap with the muzzle ready against a window or other vehicle aperture, but without the weapon projecting outside the vehicle. As soon as a threat is identified, therefore, the M4 can be pushed up and mounted in the shoulder without having to do any awkward physical maneuvers, which would likely be required with a full-length M16 rifle.

The interesting point about the M4/M4A1 is that in a sense it has shifted from being a rear-echelon or vehicular crew weapon to being a front-line infantry weapon as well, for open field and urban warfare. The extent of this switch is apparent in an article by journalist Matthew

L. Schehl published by the *Marine Corps Times* newspaper in November 2015 (Schehl 2015). Given the US Marine Corps' often proud traditionalism when it comes to small arms, we might expect some adverse reactions to the shift in M4/M4A1 roles, but in fact the opposite is the case. The author explains how Commandant General Robert Neller approved the switch, "making the M4 the primary personal weapon for Marines with infantry battalions, security forces and supporting schools by September 2016. Non-infantry Marines will continue carrying the M16A4" (Schehl 2015). This statement describes a complete swap of roles between the carbine and the rifle, with the M4 going to the front-line infantry and the M16A4 going to others. Schehl goes on to explain that "The move has proved widely popular with the Marine communities who've long complained that their legacy rifle was too long and unwieldy for urban and vehicle-borne operations in Iraq and Afghanistan. The M4 is considered by many Marines to be a tactically superior weapon to its predecessor" (Schehl 2015). Several US Marine Corps veterans clarified the reasoning behind the M4's tactical superiority. In addition to the weapon's convenience for vehicle-borne operations, the M4 offers, according to Sergeant Jonathan Ferriera, a mortarman with 1st Battalion, 8th Marines, two of the greatest attributes for an infantryman: mobility and speed. "'Size makes all the difference, because everything revolves around mobility and speed,' he said. 'The United States Marine Corps is an infantry force, and in a war of inches, everything counts'" (Schehl 2015).

One of the most telling phrases in this quotation is the reference to the "war of inches." This perfectly summarizes the experience of urban warfare that dominated much of the fighting in Iraq and Afghanistan.

Two US Marines with 2d Battalion, 8th Marine Regiment, open fire with their M4A1s during an operation in Helmand Province, Afghanistan, on July 3, 2009. With their ACOG sights they can lay down fire to 600m (656yd), although the practical effective range of the M4A1 is typically about half that distance. (Sgt. Pete Thibodeau, US Marine Corps/Wikimedia/ Public Domain)

In Iraq, the bulk of combat has been conducted in villages, towns, and cities, with Coalition troops conducting many thousands of small-unit street, building, and room-clearance operations, moving through confined spaces and making numerous shoot/don't shoot decisions under conditions of endless tension. Afghanistan has seen more varied combat terrain, including long-range firefights in which the M4/M4A1 has given, arguably, a less convincing performance (see the Impact chapter), but compound-clearance operations in winding alleyways and dark, small buildings have similarly favored the M4/M4A1's profile.

There are several specific advantages offered by the M4/M4A1 for use in urban warfare. First, it is easier to maneuver through and around narrow apertures, with a consequent reduced need for the operator to keep adjusting his body position in relation to surrounding surfaces. Second, and relating to the first point, it can be easier to achieve good muzzle control in the presence of other squad or team members, as the shorter carbine is less awkward to handle than a full-length rifle. Third, when approaching doorways, the operator should retract or raise the muzzle of the weapon so that it does not project around the door ahead of him – not to do so is an open invitation for someone on the other side of the door to grab hold of and take control of the muzzle. Having an M4/M4A1 rather than an M16 means that there is less weapon length to control, meaning the operator can move up closer to the door frame while keeping the weapon concealed. Fourth, the M4/M4A1 offers faster target acquisition and engagement at close quarters. Basic geometry dictates that the longer the weapon, the farther the muzzle has to travel to the required sight alignment across a specific interval of space. The M4/M4A1, being shorter and lighter than the M16, is quicker to snap onto a sudden target of opportunity. The difference between the two movement intervals might be measured in only fractions of a second, but such intervals can make all the difference when an opponent is also bringing his weapon to bear. Finally, the M4/M4A1 is easier to handle in a variety of shooting positions, including kneeling, prone, and side positions.

CARRYING AND MOVING

The advantages of being armed with an M4/M4A1 listed above are amplified when one considers how tactical rifle/carbine grip has changed in recent decades, and how rifles and carbines are carried. In the early decades of the M16, the system for carrying the rifle was little more than a basic two-point sling, the sling points being on the rear underside of the stock and the front underside of the forend. With this configuration, the M16 was basically carried either slung over one shoulder, flush against the soldier's back, or (for improved readiness) held out to the front in both arms but with the carrying strap running up over the right shoulder (for a right-handed shooter) to take some of the weapon's weight. Early Colt carbines featured the same carrying-strap arrangements.

During the late 1990s and the 2000s, however, the flexible marriage of tactical rails and new generations of more adjustable single-, two- and

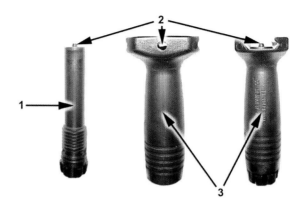

three-point slings meant that the M16 and the M4/M4A1 could be carried in better arrangements for tactical handling, particularly with the weapon mounted on the front of the torso, ready to be pulled quickly up to the shoulder for firing. The US Army's *Rifle and Carbine* manual (TC 3-22.9) states six primary weapon carry positions, specifically "hang," "safe hang," "collapsed low ready," "low ready," "high ready," and "ready" (or "ready-up"). Many of these positions are better suited to the use of the M4/M4A1 rather than the full-length M16 rifle. For example, in "collapsed low ready," the weapon is slung from the firing shoulder across the chest to the non-firing hand, the muzzle oriented down toward the floor in a safe position while the operator maintains a grip on the weapon with both hands, ready to swing the weapon upward and into the shoulder for firing. This setup is easier with the M4/M4A1, as the weapon does not interfere with the legs as much as would a free-hanging M16.

There are also advantages with a carbine when the weapon is held in a far more aggressive posture. The optimal weapon carry position for active combat, when enemy contact is imminent, is the "ready" or "ready-up" position. The weapon is up in the operator's shoulder and leveled in the general direction of the threat, the line of the muzzle only inches below the operator's eyeline, with the weapon sights permanently within his field of view. The target acquisition area is 15 degrees to the left or right of the axis of the bore. In modern tactical shooting, the ready-up position is often performed with the torso square on to the direction of movement, rather than angled with the stock shoulder back in the classic rifleman's pose. The square-on position often has the operator's non-firing hand extended well forward along the handguard; on the M4/M4A1 this grip will typically be just behind the gas block. The advantages of the square-on position for urban combat are threefold: the operator can move quickly and fluidly around the space, with a balanced stepping action; the body is naturally aligned with the threat area, reducing the time lag between visual target acquisition and target engagement; and the position of the front hand on the weapon provides a solid anchor point for the muzzle, the idea being that the operator "drives" the weapon around the combat space, the weapon essentially being an extension of his body. All the elements of this equation are more easily achieved with the M4/M4A1 carbine than with the longer M16 rifle.

Most modern troops go into combat with extensive body armor and kit, this equipment often adding several centimeters of depth from the individual's chest wall to the stock of the weapon, which in turn affects the operator's alignment with the weapon sights. The M4/M4A1's adjustable stock can compensate for this additional depth, plus the weapon's shorter overall length means that the operator can more easily maintain the extended front-hand grip.

There is also the issue of weapon weight. The basic M16 rifle weighs in the region of 7.18lb unloaded and 8.79lb loaded; adding accessories such as suppressors and underbarrel grenade launchers can dramatically increase, even nearly double, the weight of the basic weapon system. The core M4/M4A1, however, weighs 6.36lb unloaded and 6.9lb loaded, the difference with the M16 accounted for by the reduction in weight of the barrel and the stock. The difference in weight, however modest it may appear to noncombatants, can be much appreciated by a soldier who has to transport dozens of pounds of other weapons and equipment about his person.

US MILITARY ADOPTION

In the 21st century, the M4/M4A1 carbine has become almost as familiar as the AK-47 assault rifle in terms of its public profile, distribution, and prevalence on the battlefield. This is largely due to historical circumstances evolving in a manner that pushed the weapon to the fore – the GWOT from 2001 to the present day (which includes the wars in Afghanistan and Iraq) began shortly after the M4/M4A1 entered service as an official US military weapon, and the conditions of that war provided a combat environment to which the M4/M4A1 was well suited. Gathering momentum, military sales of the M4/M4A1 increased exponentially, as did export sales to a swathe of new international customers. To this picture must also be added significant civilian and law-enforcement sales (again international). Before long, the M4/M4A1 became almost synonymous with both personal and military self-defense.

As detailed earlier, the XM4 emerged from its experimental classification to be type-classified "carbine, 5.56mm, M4" on January 30, 1987; just four months later the US Marine Corps also standardized the weapon (see Rottman 2011: 43). Yet adoption of the M4 was at first tardy, at least compared to what happened a little over a decade later, partly because it was not conceived of as a mass front-line combat weapon and partly because of some of the legal wrangles outlined earlier. Initial issue of the M4/M4A1 began from 1987, but it was not until the late 1990s that the weapons began to enter service in reasonable numbers. Even then, the volumes were kept fairly small: a contract awarded to Colt on September 18, 1996, specified manufacture of just 9,785 M4s and 716 M4A1s. Most went to officers, support troops, weapons crewmen, vehicle crews, and various other auxiliary troops, the weapons being seen as something of a convenient halfway house replacement for the 9×19mm M9 Beretta pistol and the M16 rifles. The bulk of the M4/M4A1s were

US Army soldiers of the 504th Parachute Infantry Regiment set out concertina wire to maintain crowd control as residents of Vitina, Kosovo, protest in the streets on January 9, 2000. The soldier in the foreground holds an M4 carbine; operations in the Balkans in the late 1990s and early 2000s represented the first combat deployments for the M4. (Spc. Sean A. Terry, US Army/ Wikimedia/Public Domain)

taken by the US Army, but smaller numbers also went to the US Marine Corps, US Air Force, and US Navy.

It was the SOCOM community that became the motive force behind the surge in popularity of the M4/M4A1. An after-action combat evaluation of the battle between US Army Rangers and Somali insurgents in Mogadishu in 1993 found that many Rangers complained about the unwieldy nature of their M16A2s during the close-quarters urban fighting. They would have had a direct frame of comparison with the CAR-15/Colt 723s used by Delta Force operators during the same engagement, the latter weapons fitted with suppressors and combat optics. By this stage in its history, Delta Force was already wedded to various M16 carbines, purchasing CAR-15-type weapons from the commercial market, rather than official issue. According to Larry Vickers, who served with 1st SFOD-Delta during the late 1980s and the 1990s, Delta Force had standardized on the 14.5in barrel, noting that even shorter barrels resulted in the reliability and muzzle-blast issues encountered with the Colt Commando/XM177 and its ilk. They also had a variety of barrel types, either straight "pencil" or heavy cut-in barrels for mounting the M203 underbarrel grenade launcher. Post-Vietnam, CAR-15s were taken into action by special-operations forces in Panama during Operation *Just Cause* (1989–90), in the First Gulf War, and in Mogadishu in 1993, not only by Delta Force but also by other elements of SOCOM. CAR-15s became the preferred replacement for the 9×19mm Heckler & Koch MP5 submachine gun, the carbines offering full-auto firepower but with the superior performance of the 5.56×45mm cartridge.

In the US forces, it was to be the adoption and fielding of the M4 by SOCOM that would drive the weapon to new heights. (For more about SOCOM small arms see McNab 2019.) The first significant combat outing for the M4 carbine was in the hands of US Army troops deployed to Kosovo in the Balkans in 1999 (for which detailed small-arms reports seem largely absent), but it was the period of American involvement in Afghanistan and Iraq that transformed the M4's prospects.

THE M4 UNDER PRESSURE

In both Afghanistan and Iraq, SOCOM used the M4 and the M4A1 virtually as standard-issue weapons, the capabilities of the firearms enhanced by the tactical accessories within the SOPMOD packages. The stated intention of the SOPMOD kit program – to "increase operator survivability and lethality by enhanced weapon performance, target acquisition, signature suppression, and fire control" – found a perfect platform in the M4/M4A1, on account of the weapon's compact dimensions and controllable firepower. Most of SOCOM's engagements, and indeed most engagements involving the wider US armed forces in these two theaters, took place within 300m (328yd), comfortably within the M4/M4A1's effective range.

In the Development chapter above, it was noted that SOCOM's heavy use of the M4 led to a series of serious malfunctions in the weapons, largely remedied in the M4A1, and it is worth exploring a little more what the term "heavy use" implies. The accepted standard for the M4 was that it could fire 6,000 rounds before requiring a barrel replacement, but this benchmark was set with a view to the M4 being operated by non-infantry troops whose ammunition consumption would generally be far lower than front-line infantry troops in a war zone, and especially front-line SOF troops. Thus while the 6,000-round limit might have been acceptable to many troops, SOF troops in constant action and heavy firefights could easily go through three or four times that volume of ammunition with their M4s, resulting in eventual barrel blowouts. The problem of barrel endurance also manifested itself within the duration of individual firefights. On the standard M4 or early generation of the M4A1, the barrel could reach its "transition temperature" – essentially the point at which the barrel loses its structural integrity – at $c.1,400$–$1,500°F$, which could be reached after going through about 11–12 magazines rapidly. For most of the US troops, this was not a problem, unless they were caught in an unexpectedly intense firefight. Veterans' forums speak of a standard magazine load for a combat patrol of six magazines in pouches and one magazine in the weapon, each magazine holding 30 rounds. (As an aside, in many armies the standard practice is to avoid filling magazines to their maximum capacity, partly because it increases the chances of feed and extraction problems, and partly because over time it weakens the magazine spring. The US military, however, has

US Army Specialist Ian Bucklin fires his M4 carbine during partnered marksmanship live-fire training on Tactical Base Gamberi in eastern Afghanistan, May 29, 2015. In addition to his ACOG optic, his weapon is fitted with the AN/PEQ-15 ATPIAL system. (DOD)

in recent years used a high percentage of cheap, single-use magazines, which has meant reduced consideration of matters such as magazine wear and filling to full 30-round capacity.) At a 30-round loading, the seven magazines or "basic load" give a total of 210 rounds – well short of the *c*.348 rounds of 12 magazines. Thus, even with an extra two magazines (a common addition to an infantry load in Afghanistan and Iraq), the infantryman was in little danger of running his M4 to the transition temperature.

For SOCOM operators, by contrast, the limitation of the 210-round basic load was frequently exceeded. On public domain forums, some SOF veterans speak of carrying "double basic load" – 13 magazines (12 in bags and pouches and one in the weapon) – or even as many as 15–20 magazines, on missions where they were confident of facing heavy and prolonged fighting, often without reinforcement. These magazines could be gone through very rapidly in a demanding firefight, on account of the number of enemy to be engaged, the time-intensity of the threat or operation, and also tactical preferences. For example, in SOCOM small-unit tactics, during a fireteam (four men) or squad (up to ten men) extraction, two operators might take up fixed positions and provide relentless fire from their M4s, aiming to achieve some measure of fire superiority while their comrades pulled back under the covering fire. Using up their magazines rapidly, the troops would therefore use the carbines, in effect, as light support weapons (LSWs) in the absence of heavier firepower. These tactics were viable once the heavier barrels and improved bolts were available, but the lighter barrels and older bolts could be pushed to the transition temperature in short order.

THE BATTLE OF WANAT

The battle of Wanat, fought on July 13, 2008, in Nuristan Province, Afghanistan, offers a critical insight into the nature of the early M4 reliability issues, once the weapons were pushed beyond their limits. It also demonstrates that it was not only SOCOM troops who might be compelled to fire their M4s to the point of destruction.

Vehicle Patrol Base (VPB) Kahler, accompanied by a separate observation post called OP Topside about 50m (55yd) beyond the perimeter of the main base, was established near Wanat on July 8, one of several similar bases built in the region for the purpose of disrupting supplies flowing to the Taliban from the Federally Administered Tribal Regions of Pakistan. By July 13, the force consisted of 48 US Army soldiers from the 503d Infantry Regiment (Airborne) and 173d Airborne Brigade Combat Team and 24 soldiers serving in the Afghan National Army (ANA). The weapons and equipment included five M1114 Humvees: one mounting a TOW missile launcher, two others mounting .50-cal. M2HB heavy machine guns, and the remaining two fitted with Mk 19 automatic grenade launchers. In terms of small arms, the weapons were M4 carbines, M249 SAW (the primary fireteam LSW), and 7.62×51mm M240 machine guns.

VPB Kahler was set in a field about 300m (328yd) long by 100m (109yd) wide, with high ground surrounding it. During the five days before the battle, the base was made more defensible through the digging of field fortifications, laying of barbed wire, and building of HESCO blast barriers, but the defenses were not complete, owing to the lack of time and the breakdown of a Bobcat utility vehicle. Thus this isolated outpost,

A soldier loads a 40mm grenade into his M203A2 underbarrel grenade launcher. Note how the grenade-launcher mount fits into the step in the heavy barrel. The ladder sight on the top rail can be ranged out to 250m (273yd). (347karlovo/ Wikimedia/ CC BY-SA 3.0)

manned by a small force with few heavy weapons, was acutely vulnerable when, at about 0230hrs on the morning of July 13, 200–500 Taliban fighters attacked.

This was not an improvised attack, but was rather a carefully planned and coordinated operation involving several Taliban groups. For several days before the attack, the US troops had observed suspicious figures beyond the wire observing the positions and personnel of the base. Local Afghan civilians had warned the US troops that the base was vulnerable and that an attack was imminent. When the onslaught finally came, the base fell under a concentrated storm of small-arms and rocket-propelled grenade (RPG) fire from prepared firing positions. The fire was intelligently directed. It quickly knocked out the 120mm mortar and the TOW-mounted Humvee, taking away much of the base's organic heavy weapons in minutes, and also bringing the base Command Post (CP) under direct fire.

Straight away the US troops began to take casualties. Four men were killed in the first 20 minutes alone, and three seriously wounded. Small arms, plus the Mk 19s and the M2HBs, became the key weapons in repelling the attack. The M249, M240, and M2HBs and Mk 19s could put down effective fire to 600m (656yd) and beyond, but the combat was frequently at much closer ranges, in some cases right up to the barbed wire. Those troops armed with M4s raced through their ammunition supplies as they desperately attempted to achieve localized fire superiority and keep the enemy at bay. An official account of the battle, written by the US Army Combat Studies Institute, explains how the mortarmen, now without their principal weapon, had to fall back on the 5.56mm M4:

> When the action began, the two engineers who were operating the Bobcat next to the mortar area reinforced [Staff Sergeant Erich] Phillips' men in the mortar pit. There, the defenders used whatever weapons were available to them, firing personal weapons furiously into the nearby trees and aiming 40-mm grenades at more distant enemy positions. Without any machine guns of their own, the mortarmen had to use M4 assault rifles firing at the maximum rate of fire simply to suppress the enemy in order to survive. In this way, Phillips burned out a series of three M4s. He then picked up an M249 SAW belonging to the engineers and tried to fire it but it failed to shoot. Mortarman [Jesse] Queck had previously tried to fire the SAW but it was jammed. Another trooper later fired it successfully after changing its barrel. Queck instead fired an AT-4 rocket launcher he found at one of the buildings from which enemy fire was coming. Soldiers nearby followed up Queck's effort with hand grenades. (US Army CSI 2010: 144)

The picture here is one of desperation. The sheer intensity of fire is indicated by the astonishing fact that Phillips alone fired three M4s until each weapon was destroyed, indicating that during his handling of these weapons he personally fired what would have been in excess of 1,000 rounds of 5.56×45mm ammunition. It should also be noted that many of

the other M4s experienced failures; both SAWs and the Mk 19s also suffered from a significant number of stoppages.

A more quantifiable indication of the levels of demand placed upon the M4s comes from the battle for the "Crow's Nest," the highest position on the base. It had an M240 machine gun manned by Corporal Jonathan R. Ayers, Specialist Christopher McKaig, and Specialist Pruitt Rainey. After ripping through multiple belts of 7.62×51mm ammunition, the M240 finally ran out of ammunition belts:

> With their M240 effectively out of action, Ayers and McKaig continued the fight at the Crow's Nest with two M4 carbines. Their technique was to pop up together at intervals, fire six to nine rounds at the muzzle flashes ringing the OP, then drop down before the enemy could respond. Although scared, the pair continued this maneuver until enemy return fire struck and killed Ayers, who collapsed over his weapon. Now alone in the position, McKaig began to experience problems with his M4. "My weapon was overheating. I had shot about 12 magazines by this point already and it had only been about a half hour or so into the fight. I couldn't charge my weapon and put another round in because it was too hot, so I got mad and threw my weapon down." When he tried to use Ayers' rifle, he discovered that an AK-47 round had disabled it in the same volley that had killed his squad mate. (US Army CSI 2010: 155)

Two key points are evident from this account. The first is that it gives a sense of the accuracy of the M4 as a weapon, the operators putting down

A US soldier with the 1st Battalion, 32d Infantry Regiment, 10th Mountain Division, lays down fire from his M4 carbine in Barge Matal, Afghanistan, during Operation *Mountain Fire* on July 12, 2009. (US Army Sergeant Matthew C. Moeller, 5th Mobile Public Affairs Detachment/Wikimedia/Public Domain)

small bursts of fire onto muzzle-flash targets before resuming cover. This type of controlled semi-auto fire, rather than long sustained bursts of full-auto fire, is really the best use of the M4. Despite the judicious use of controlled fire, however, McKaig still burns through tremendous amounts of ammunition. At 12 magazines his now super-heated weapon goes into shutdown, the whole firearm seizing up like an automobile that has run out of oil and coolant. With his dead comrade's M4 out of service owing to the impact of an AK-47 round, McKaig subsequently stayed in the fight by detonating two Claymore mines positioned just outside OP Topside.

The battle of Wanat raged for about four hours, during which time nine US Army soldiers were killed and 27 wounded, and four ANA soldiers wounded. VPB Kahler was only saved by the trenchant defense of the soldiers within it, but also by the steady increase of American support fire, from regional tube artillery and attack helicopters. By the time the Taliban insurgents withdrew, they had lost up anywhere between 21 and 65 dead (the numbers are unclear) and c.45 wounded.

Although the battle can hardly be said to have been won or lost by either side, some of the press and various specialists pounced on the action as an American defeat, on account of the heavy losses incurred. The M4 also came in for close scrutiny. The issue of the M4's reliability will be considered in further depth in the Impact chapter below, but here it is worth quoting from the Combat Studies Institute report on the evaluation of the M4. The report's authors reflect on the gap between the original design purpose of the M4 and its *in extremis* application at Wanat:

> The concept of employment of weapons in an infantry platoon directed crew-served weapons to provide high rates of fire capable of suppressing enemy positions. These weapons, M240 machine guns and SAWs especially, were designed for such use and were equipped with belt-fed ammunition and extra barrels. No M240s failed in the action and the SAWs that jammed, did so after firing a great number of rounds. As noted above, these jams were fixed when the operators changed barrels. In fact, most of the weapons that jammed at Wanat were M4 carbines. The M4 was the basic individual weapon carried by US Soldiers in Afghanistan and was not designed to fire at the maximum or cyclic rate for extended periods. Enemy action and weapons dispositions forced the defenders of COP [Combat Outpost, an alternative name for this VPB] Kahler and OP Topside to use their M4s in uncharacteristic roles. This, not weapons maintenance deficiencies or inherent weaknesses in weapons design, was the reason a number of weapons jammed during the battle. The maintenance of a high rate of fire was critical to retaining fire superiority and to prevent positions (particularly OP Topside) from being overrun by determined and continuous insurgent assaults. (US Army CSI 2010: 219–220)

The CSI report's view is that at Wanat the M4 was pushed well beyond foreseen limits for this type of weapon. Unlike the M249 SAW, which had

a barrel-change facility, the M4's fixed barrel meant that once it reached the critical transition temperature, only a visit to the unit armory for a barrel replacement could get the weapon going again. The "determined and continuous insurgent assaults" forced the soldiers to use their M4s in "uncharacteristic roles," specifically the laying down of rapid semi-auto and full-auto suppressive fire against multiple and widely dispersed area targets.

An M4A1 in combat configuration in Afghanistan in 2013. The combined tactical foregrip/bipod, fitted to the underside of the RAS rail, has become an increasingly popular attachment; with the bipod deployed, the operator has a more stable platform for distance shooting. (DIBYANGSHU SARKAR/AFP via Getty Images)

Firefight, US Army 10th Mountain Division, Afghanistan (overleaf)

Here a four-man fireteam from the 10th Mountain Division conduct a classic fire-and-maneuver response to a Taliban ambush in Nuristan Province, Afghanistan, in 2008. Three of the men are armed with the M4A1 carbine, accessorized primarily with the ACOG close-combat optic and the AN/PEQ-2 ITPIAL aiming device on the handguard; one of the soldiers also has a tactical weapon light, which can be useful when transitioning into darkened buildings or if the operation runs on into the nighttime hours. One of the fireteam has the M249 Squad Automatic Weapon (SAW) – an American military variant of the Belgian FN Minimi – to provide the team with organic fire support. He has taken up a covering position and is pouring 5.56mm fire onto elevated enemy positions approximately 200m (219yd) away. While the maximum recommended practical (not cyclical) sustained rate of fire for an M4/M4A1 is c.12–15rd/min, the SAW is able to put down c.50rd/min, on account of its barrel-change feature. While one of the soldiers is changing the magazine on his M4A1, another is putting down his own covering fire as the squad leader rushes forward.

EXPANDED USE

As we shall see in the Impact chapter, the reliability issues of the M4 carbine have not been forgotten. Indeed, the ultimate conclusions of the CSI report have even been contested by one of its authors. Certainly, the experience at Wanat was not a one-off incident. Both SOCOM and regular US soldiers on occasions experienced serious M4 weapon malfunctions due to excessive firing, extreme environmental effects, or to the wear-and-tear that accompany all service weapons. In the SOCOM context, some experts have also pointed out that troops might go into action with the same M4s issued during training. Given the thousands of rounds a typical SOF operator puts through firearms during training, an individual M4 might be reaching the end of its barrel life even before it is taken into combat – one of the reasons why some authorities have recommended that the weapons be fitted with shot counters.

Given these problems, how did the M4/M4A1 carbine become *the* dominant firearm in US military use, both proven and popular among US troops? A central reason was that the M4A1, itself improved during its lifespan, solved many (but not all, according to some) of the reliability issues associated with the M4. With its new barrel, improved bolt, and intelligent range of accessories, the M4A1 could deliver rapid fire well

US soldiers from Charlie Company, 2d Battalion, 22d Infantry Regiment, 1st Brigade Combat Team, 10th Mountain Division along the Zaghytun Chay River, Iraq, in 2007. Each soldier has fitted his M4 carbine with an M68 CCO and a tactical flashlight. The latter, and the large backpacks, suggest an overnight operation. (Camera Operator: STAFF SGT. SAMUEL BENDET (US Air Force)/Wikimedia/ Public Domain)

in excess of 12 magazines and was perfectly suited to the needs of Military Operations in Urban Terrain (MOUT) and the short- to medium-range encounters that seemed most characteristic of infantry combat in the early 20th century. From 2010, the shift to the M4A1 became inexorable. By September of that year, the US Army had ordered 12,000 conversion kits to enable M4s to be upgraded to SOCOM M4A1 standard, with another 65,000 conversion kits and 25,000 new M4A1 purchases for 2011. Then, in 2012, the US Army revealed the extent of its intentions by placing an order for 120,000 new M4A1s with FN Herstal, after an acrimonious bid process in which the contract was first awarded to Remington, but passed to FN Herstal after a series of legal wrangles between the US Army, Remington, and Colt. In 2015 Colt Defense began sharing the contract with FN Herstal. In many ways, the M4A1 could now be regarded as the standard-issue US infantry combat weapon.

Bringing the story up to date, in March 2019 the US Army Contracting Command at Picatinny Arsenal posted a solicitation for 167,195 further M4 and M4A1 carbines; the contract was awarded to FN America in February 2020. In total, the US Army has acquired more than 500,000 M4/M4A1 carbines since the weapon was developed in the late 1990s. The US Marine Corps was more resistant to the concept of the M4/M4A1, but in 2015, as explained above, General Robert Neller announced the wholesale adoption of the M4A1 into the Corps.

The M4/M4A1 has also had an interesting life within the US Navy and US Air Force. In the Navy, the M4A1 and Mk 18 CQBR are issued to vehicle crews and to naval SOF, including the US Navy SEALs and various

US Marines from the 24th Marine Expeditionary Unit conduct VBSS training. The blue barrels indicate that the carbines have been configured for the Special Effects Small Arms Marking Systems (SESAMS) Kit, better known as "Simunitions." (Gunnery Sgt. James H. Frank/USMC/ Wikimedia/Public Domain)

US Navy and Marine Corps units that conduct Visit, Board, Search, and Seizure (VBSS) operations, or its helicopter fast-roping version: Helicopter Visit, Board, Search, and Seizure (HVBSS). The Mk 18 CQBR is particularly suited to the very-close-quarters action involved in ship boardings, where combat ranges can be measured in a handful of yards. One important consideration in such actions (also in hostage-rescue missions) is over-penetration of the round, i.e. the bullet passing through the intended target and subsequently endangering noncombatants or comrades. Inside a ship this situation is especially problematic, in that the surrounding metal surfaces provide a perfect environment for generating wild ricochets. For this reason, VBSS teams often use frangible ammunition, such as the 5.56×45mm Reduced Ricochet Limited Penetration (RRLP), Mk 255 Mod 0. This cartridge has a 62-grain jacketed frangible projectile with an effective range of about 100m (109yd), is highly water resistant, and if it hits a solid surface breaks apart with limited lethal fragmentation. A presentation delivered by Sung Y. Kim of the Small Arms Ammunition Branch, Crane Division, NSWC-Crane in 2006 noted the key results of ricochet and splatter tests. With respect to ricochet fragments, "No fragments penetrated deeper than 2.5" into 10% (by weight) Ballistic Gelatin after 45° impact on AR500 steel plate located 15 ft. from the muzzle," while there was "No reverse splatter toward the shooter position from AR500 steel plate 15 ft. away from the muzzle" (Kim 2006: 10). Although standing in the immediate vicinity of these impacting rounds could hardly be described as "safe," the use of frangible rounds dramatically reduces the risk of unintentional injuries inflicted on oneself or others.

The US Air Force is also a major user of the M4 carbine. Having relied for many years upon M16 variants as its primary firearm (indeed it was the first adopter of the M16), the Air Force in June 2019 switched most of its purchase and training focus to the M4 carbine, standardizing with the shift among most of the rest of the US military. An interesting development within this change of focus has been the creation and production of the GAU-5A variant of the M4, announced via the media in 2019. The GAU-5A is essentially a heavily modified M4 carbine, designed to be broken down into two parts and stored inside the seat kit of ACES II ejection seats on modern jets. Intended as a survival and self-defense weapon with more potency than the pilots' usual M9 Beretta pistol, it was designed by the Air Force Gunsmith Shop at Lackland AFB, Texas, to meet a requirement for a gun that from its stored state could be put together within 30 seconds and could accurately engage a human-sized target out to 200m (219yd). The GAU-5A has replaced the M4's 14.5in barrel with a shorter 12.5in barrel, and the designers installed a Cry Havoc Tactical Quick Release Barrel (QRB) kit, which enables both the barrel and the front handguard to be removed as a single unit. Other fittings and modifications include an M4-style collapsible stock, flip-up BUIS, and an Israeli FAB Defense AGF-43S folding pistol grip.

INTERNATIONAL USE

The bulk of our focus in any analysis of the M4/M4A1 naturally focuses on the United States, the country responsible for the development of the M4 carbine and by far the largest user and innovator of the weapon system. Yet the M4 carbine has achieved vast export success. In fact,

Royal Danish Army military police officers conduct advanced law-enforcement training involving high-risk arrest scenarios at the Grafenwöhr Training Area in Germany, September 22, 2009. Note the loops on the bottom of the magazines to aid withdrawal of the latter from the ammunition pouches and magazine well. (Gertrud Zach, US Army Wikimedia/Public Domain)

The M4 carbine has a truly international distribution. Here an M4-armed Georgian Special Operations Forces soldier with Scouts Platoon, Delta Company, Special Mountain Battalion, conducts a reconnaissance operation on February 14, 2014, during Georgian Mission Rehearsal Exercise 14-02B at the Joint Multinational Readiness Center in Hohenfels, Germany. (SPC Brian Rankin/Public domain photograph from defenseimagery.mil)

looking through the list of M4 adopters, it requires some effort to find a country that has not purchased the M4/M4A1 to any degree. The M4/M4A1's versatility as a CQB weapon has made it particularly popular among international SOF and elite police units, but it is also used by regular infantry and military personnel around the world. It is impossible here to explain the use by each particular country, but some instances can be noted.

First, the M4/M4A1 is built under license by several countries for their armed forces. The biggest producer of non-US licensed M4-type weapons is Canada, via Colt Canada (formerly Diemaco, until 2005). The standard rifles of the Canadian Army have been the C7, C7A1 (Diemaco C7FT), and C7A2, modified derivations of the M16A1 and M16A2 rifles, while the C8 and its sub-variants offer the carbine models. The C8 is not a direct M4 copy, however; rather, it is more based on the Colt 653, or M16A1 carbine. Like the C7 rifle, the C8 carbine features higher-quality components in some aspects, but it essentially has the same schematic layout, performance, and operating characteristics as the M4A1. The C8 has itself spawned multiple sub-variants, including: the C8A1 with flat-top upper receiver and C79 optical sight; the C8A2 with a heavier cold-hammer-forged barrel; the C8SFW (Special Forces Weapon) with a 15.7in heavy-profile barrel and a special fitting for mounting bayonets and grenade launchers; the C8FTHB (Flat Top Heavy Barrel) with a barrel cut-out for mounting the M203 underbarrel grenade launcher; the C8A3 with ambidextrous controls and improved rail systems; and the C8CT (Custom Tactical) with a 16in free-floating barrel, two-stage match trigger, specially weighted furniture, and improved ergonomic adjustability, all to suit the Designated Marksman role.

Other licensed producers of the M4 are Malaysia and Turkey. Malaysia acquired the rights to produce M4s in 2006–07, 14,000 weapons being manufactured by SME Ordnance Sdn Bhd (SMEO) to replace the Steyr AUG assault rifle as the standard Malaysian Army service rifle. China, meanwhile, manufactures an unlicensed copy of the M4A1. Known as the CQ 5.56mm Type A assault carbine, it entered production around 2006 and is manufactured by Norinco. Used internally by select Chinese SOF and SWAT-style law-enforcement units, the CQ Type A has also achieved military export sales to Paraguay and (in a semiautomatic version) to civilian shooters in Italy, Ukraine, South Africa, and Canada.

In terms of M4/M4A1s purchased directly from the United States, some of the major purchasers include Afghanistan, Argentina, Colombia, Hungary, Iraq, Israel, Japan, Pakistan, the Philippines, and Singapore, many of the deals part of Foreign Military Sales (FMS) packages. Afghanistan and Iraq have received large volumes of M4/M4A1s – understandably so, given the huge investment of US forces in developing the infrastructure and capability of both the Afghan National Army and

Police in Mumbai, India, handle a collection of police firearms, including the Colt M4 carbine with the heavy barrel. (Kunal Patil/Hindustan Times via Getty Images)

the Iraqi Army since 2001. In 2008, for example, the Government of Iraq requested 80,000 M16A4s, 25,000 M4 carbines, 2,550 M203 underbarrel grenade launchers, plus all the necessary spare parts, support equipment, publications and technical data, personnel training and training equipment, contractor engineering and technical support services, and logistics support (Defense Security Cooperation Agency 2008).

One of the largest users from the list, however, is Israel. Its adoption is worth a closer look, not least because the Israel Defense Forces (IDF) have given the M4A1 (the main variant it acquired) extensive combat testing in both its regular army and SOF. The author has been unable to find the exact numbers of M4s and M4A1s exported to Israel for IDF use, but they have certainly been acquired in the many tens of thousands, alongside more than 100,000 M16-type rifles. The IDF M4A1s have seen action many times over the last 18 years or so, principally in operations in the Gaza Strip, including Operation *Defensive Shield* (2002), Operation

An Armed Forces of the Philippines Joint Special Operations Group soldier and an Australian Army 2nd Commando Regiment soldier clear a room during close-quarters battle training, 2017. The Australian soldier's M4A1 carbine, extremely heavily accessorized, contrasts with the training M4 used by the Filipino soldier. (US Army Staff Sergeant Kwadwo Frimpong/ Wikimedia/Public Domain)

An Israeli soldier, his M4 fitted with a rubber-bullet firing attachment and a Meprolight Mepro M21 reflex optic, aims his weapon toward Palestinians during clashes in the West Bank city of Ramallah, 2014. (Issam Rimawi/Anadolu Agency/Getty Images)

Cast Lead (2008–09), and Operation *Protective Edge* (2014). As well as US-type accessories, the IDF M4A1s are often fitted with the Meprolight Mepro M21 Self-Illuminated Reflex Sight, a very robust 1× magnification red-dot sight. This Israeli-produced sight is designed to work without the need for battery power; it utilizes a fiber-optic collector system for day use and a miniature self-powered tritium light source at night. It is also configured to be used easily with NVGs and for shooting with both eyes open – a key feature of reflexive shooting. Other fittings used on IDF M4A1s include a special rubber-bullet firing attachment, which consists of a metal tube that fits over the muzzle brake (at first glance it looks something akin to a slim suppressor). A rubber bullet is inserted into the tube, and is then fired via a blank cartridge; such devices have been heavily used during riot-control actions in Gaza.

Israel Defense Forces paratroopers, Gaza Strip (opposite)

Here, three IDF paratroopers engage in an urban firefight with Hamas insurgents in the Gaza Strip during Operation *Cast Lead* (also known as the Gaza War) in January 2009. All three soldiers are armed with M4A1 carbines, one of several standard-issue weapons for both regular infantry and SOF units in the IDF. The soldiers are, however, in quite different stages of operating their weapons: The soldier in the foreground is in the process of clearing a weapon malfunction, in this case a failure to fire. He follows the standard quick-clearance drill: safety on; check the magazine is seated properly; rack the charging handle to clear the unspent cartridge; return to operation. The soldier in the center has no such trouble and is firing the carbine in semi-auto mode, using his Meprolight Mepro M21 reflex optic (a standard IDF tactical accessory) to engage targets about 200m (219yd) away. The third soldier, meanwhile, has fired a 40mm grenade down the street from his M203 underbarrel launcher. He is aiming the weapon via the flip-up leaf sight atop the handguard, the sight having 10m (11yd) and 50m (55yd) adjustment increments; the front sight post serves as the front aiming post.

A masked Hezbollah fighter displays an M4 carbine that he claims was taken from a dead Israeli soldier in Aita Ech Chaab, southern Lebanon, 2006. (Michael Appleton/NY Daily News Archive via Getty Images)

In the hands of well-trained users, IDF M4A1s have given reliable service. Certainly, there does not appear to be any systematic critical combat feedback regarding the M4A1 in battle, even when used by some of Israel's most elite SOF units. Yet, since 2001 the IDF had steadily moved to replace its M4A1s and M16A4s with an indigenous weapon, the bullpup 5.56×45mm Israel Weapon Industries (IWI) Tavor. The reasons for the replacement vary a little depending on the source, but many focus upon politics and domestic economy, the argument being that the IDF prefers home-produced weapons rather than foreign imports. An article by IWI, however – admittedly the designer of the Tavor – explains in more detail the chronology and the thinking behind the move to the Tavor. Between November 2001 and March 2002, the Tavor and the M4 underwent a series of punishing combat trials, focusing on determining which weapon performed best in the following six categories: mean rounds between failures (MRBF); accuracy and retention of zero; user ergonomics over extended periods of use; speed and accuracy of sighting in daytime and nighttime, from iron sights to advanced optics and other aiming accessories; use with the M203 underbarrel grenade launcher; and maintenance-relevant issues.

In these trials, the Tavor apparently emerged as the winner. The reasons given for its success were fourfold. First, the bullpup design gave the Tavor a shorter overall length (the TAR-21 measures 28.3in) but with a full-length rifle barrel of 18in, delivering higher velocities and superior ballistic performance. Second, despite being heavier than the basic M4 – the TAR-21 weighs 7.21lb – the Tavor pushes most of its weight to the rear of the firearm, closer to the operator's center of gravity, thus making the weapon easier to handle and less tiring to carry (according to its advocates). Third, tactical reloads can be performed without taking the hand off the pistol grip and without having to break cheek weld. Finally, in terms of reliability, the Tavor has a sealed operating mechanism, making it highly resistant to malfunctions caused by the ingress of dirt, dust, sand, mud, and other foreign objects. It also has a long-stroke piston mechanism rather than the direct-impingement system of the M4; proponents say that this mechanism is far more reliable.

In November 2009, the IWI Tavor X95 or "Micro-Tavor" was selected to be the future standard rifle of the IDF. The X95 is an even more compact version of TAR-21, with relatively straightforward caliber conversion features.

The M4/M4A1 will doubtless stay in IDF hands, giving good service, for many years to come as the IDF transitions to the Tavor X95. The IDF decision to adopt the Tavor, however, prompts a discussion about the impact of the M4/M4A1, and its future. This discussion takes us into the heart of the criticisms and defenses of the M4/M4A1, and also compels an evaluation of the weapon in a changing field of military firearms.

IMPACT
Battlefield evaluation

On one level, the impact of the M4/M4A1 is not to be questioned: it has been a primary battlefield weapon in the longest period of continuous warfare in US history. If we widen the scope to include all the world's M4/M4A1 users, including law-enforcement and even civilian users, then the impact of the carbine is even greater. In US law enforcement alone, M4 carbines (produced and modified by a variety of manufacturers) are the weapon of choice for most SWAT-type units, and often grace the trunks or interiors of armed-response squad cars. For civilians, the M4 is a weapon of choice for those wanting a carbine home-defense weapon, with the strong market demand reflected in hefty price tags.

In an example of the M4's modularity, this weapon is fitted with a 40mm M320 underbarrel grenade launcher, the M320's electronic targeting system visible on the left side of the handguard. The weapon's effective range against an area target is 350m (383yd). (Photo courtesy of PEO Soldier/Wikimedia/Public Domain)

A US police officer tests out night-vision optics for an M4 carbine. The optics are here mounted upon a blue plastic training weapon. These training models, made from impact-resistant polyurethane construction with steel reinforcement, have all the handling features of the real weapons and can also mount accessories. (Spencer Platt/Getty Images)

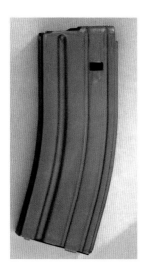

The standard STANAG 30-round magazine. These magazines need to be treated with care, as they are easily damaged. (M62/Wikimedia/CC BY-SA 3.0)

On the individual human level, furthermore, we can certainly say that the M4/M4A1's impact has frequently been profound. A single incident, no greater or lesser than thousands of others that have occurred in the GWOT, illustrates the point. In March 2005, a Coalition convoy traveling through Iraq, protected by three Humvees carrying Military Police (MPs) from the Kentucky National Guard, came under a sudden heavy ambush, initiated when an RPG knocked out the lead Humvee in the unit. Several troops dismounted from the rear vehicle to fight, but were quickly wounded by incoming small-arms fire. With chaos threatening, two of the MPs dismounted, one them (a squad-leader staff sergeant) armed with an M4 and two hand grenades and the other (a team-leader sergeant) with an M4 fitted with an M203 underbarrel grenade launcher. With support fire from .50-cal. and 5.56mm machine guns, the two individuals closed up to the ditches in which the enemy were positioned, and started clearing them systematically with their carbines. Such was the intensity of the ensuing firefight that the team-leader sergeant even had to sprint back to the vehicles for extra magazines and three more M203 grenades. The team-leader sergeant alone killed four enemy combatants with aimed M4 shots; the total enemy death toll (from all causes, including suppressive automatic fire) was 24, with a further six wounded.

The total active US combatants in this action were seven MPs (Burden 2006: 171–74). There is little doubt that for them, the M4 was, for a few short minutes, the most important piece of technology in their lives. That it worked is attested to by the results of the action.

Nevertheless, as the Introduction to this book acknowledged, the reputation of the M4/M4A1 is a matter of some dispute, depending on the source. For much of the rest of this book, therefore, we will try to assess the impact of the M4/M4A1 through the prism of this dispute. For there are some who contest that the carbine's battlefield impact has at best been indifferent, but at worst cost lives.

RELIABILITY

The issue of reliability has already been addressed to a degree in the context of the battle of Wanat and the SOCOM upgrades that prompted the evolution of the M4A1. From Wanat, we read the defense of the M4 on the grounds that the critical stoppages in extreme firefights occurred when the carbine was being put through levels of demand for which it was simply not designed. This defense has not been allowed to stand, however. In February 2014, *The Washington Times* released a major two-part report into what its author, Rowan Scarborough, saw as the critical failings of the M4 carbine (Scarborough 2014a & 2014b). Based on Pentagon documents and interviews with front-line troops, the report does confirm some of the elements already noted in this book, most notably that the original lightweight M4 barrel was unsuited to use in intensive firefights. Scarborough compellingly adds, however, many sources that question the M4's very operating mechanism, seeing it as difficult and fiddly to maintain properly in the field, prone to heavy fouling because of its direct-impingement mechanism, and with faulty trigger mechanisms (likely issues with the three-round-burst function).

Most damningly, Scarborough includes statements from Douglas R. Cubbison, the principal author of the CSI Wanat report, who alleges that the statement "This, not weapons maintenance deficiencies or inherent weaknesses in weapons design, was the reason a number of weapons jammed during the battle" was not his conclusion, but a later Army insertion. Cubbison, and several other US military authorities referenced, argue that the M4 was simply not the right tool for modern warfare. Several SOCOM operators said that they only came to trust the M4 after performing custom upgrades, especially to trigger groups and barrels. Poor-quality magazines seemed a genuine problem, the standard-issue US military magazines often failing because of weakened springs. When troops used high-quality privately purchased magazines, however, many of these particular problems disappeared.

Overall, Scarborough's well-researched report depicts the M4 as a weapon with at least some question marks associated with it. Civilian authors, myself included, who have never had to hang their lives on a weapon nor fire a single weapon to the point of destruction, tread warily into these arguments. Certainly, at the time of writing, the reputation of the modern M4A1 in particular seems reasonably high among both veterans and many analysts. Systematic distrust of a weapon tends to have a pervasive feedback, but I have found little of that. I note also how so many former SOF operators have gone on to purchase M4 carbines as their weapon of choice in civilian life; this would be a strange investment (especially with such a hefty price tag) if the weapon was poorly regarded, although the civilian market does allow individuals to make all manner of modifications to take the weapon to the desired specification.

Complicating the matter are the various US military surveys that indicate widespread approval for the M4. One of the key surveys in this regard was that written by Sara M. Russell and published by the CNA Corporation. Titled *Soldier Perspectives on Small Arms in Combat* (Russell 2006), the report's methodology was to conduct more than 2,600 surveys with soldiers returning from Iraq or Afghanistan within the previous 12 months "and had engaged in a firefight using the M9, M4, M16 (A2 or A4), or M249 during their last deployment" (Russell 2006: 1). The survey focused on questions of weapon function, reliability, durability, training, maintenance, cleaning, stoppages, accessories, and environment.

The headline result was that the M4 carbine came out with the highest overall satisfaction score, an impressive 89 percent. This was significantly higher than the other weapon types, with the M16 rifle at 75 percent, the M249 SAW at 71 percent, and the M9 pistol at a demoralizing 58 percent. Beyond the overall score, the survey asked the soldiers to rate their levels of satisfaction in the following areas: ammunition (79 percent); handling (90 percent); accuracy (94 percent); range (92 percent); rate of fire (93 percent); training (85 percent); maintainability (87 percent); cleaning equipment (75 percent); corrosion resistance (80 percent); accessories (86 percent) (Russell 2006: 12). These are high scores indeed, and in only

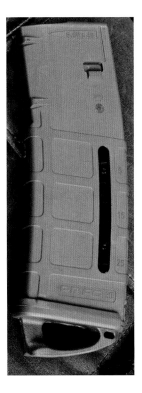

A close-up of the Magpul PMAG Gen M2 polymer magazine. The use of such high-quality magazines can dramatically reduce the numbers of weapon stoppages in the M4/M4A1. (Joe Cereghino/Wikimedia/ CC BY 2.0)

one category did another weapon score higher: the M249 SAW was given 94 percent for its rate of fire. It is interesting that the qualities most pertinent to combat performance – handling, accuracy, range, and rate of fire – are the four categories in which the M4 scored in the 90+ percent category, belying the reports of poor reliability described earlier. Russell did, however, provide additional explanations about the reliability of the M4 and the other weapons in the field:

> Reports of weapon stoppages at least one time while engaging the enemy were 30 percent or less across all weapons. Most stoppages were reported to have a small impact on continuing in the engagement with the weapon. The M9 and M249 were reported to have the most stoppages and the highest resulting negative impact. In most cases, attaching accessories using methods of attachment other than rails has negative impact with regard to weapon stoppages, repairs, and confidence in reliability and durability. For the M4, M16, and M249, firing in semi-automatic mode resulted in positive effects, such as decreasing repairs and stoppages, as well as increasing soldier levels of confidence in weapon reliability and durability.
>
> Soldiers issued cleaning kits were less likely to experience stoppages and more likely to be confident in weapon reliability. Weapon cleaning type and frequency had little impact on stoppages and repairs overall. However, soldiers who frequently performed quick wipe-down cleanings experienced more stoppages. Frequency of disassembled cleanings had no effect on the occurrence of stoppages. Variations in lubrication practices, such as type of lubrication used and amount of

Maritime Raiding Force, Gulf of Aden (opposite)

Here a small unit of the US Marine Corps' Maritime Raiding Force (MRF) perform a Visit, Board, Search, and Seizure (VBSS) operation in the Gulf of Aden *c.*2011, moving carefully up the main external stairway to the bridge. They have the M4/M4A1 as their weapon of choice, the compact dimensions inside and around ships making the carbine particularly suitable for convenient movement up the steep stairs and through the narrow passageways. The men here are all equipped with M4A1s with ACOG optics, although the MRF also frequently use red-dot reflex sights such as the EOTech 553 HOLOgraphic Weapon Sight. They also have the EOTech LA-5/PEQ ATPIAL aiming device mounted on the top of the handguard, just behind the front sight. This unit delivers either a visible aiming laser, infrared aiming laser, or infrared illuminator, giving the operator a spectrum of options as he moves from bright sun-drenched deck to dark lower levels. The Marines move cautiously up the stairs, covering doorways and platforms as they advance. The most high-profile VBSS mission conducted by the MRF began on September 8, 2010, when the container ship M/V *Magellan Star*, with 11 crew members on board, was hijacked by nine armed Somali pirates. The next day, the ship was taken back by a force of 24 Marines, members of the 15th Marine Expeditionary Unit's Maritime Raiding Force, who deployed by helicopter and small boats from the amphibious transport dock USS *Dubuque* (LPD-8). No shots were actually fired during the mission (although stun grenades were deployed) and all the hostages were freed unharmed.

lubrication applied, also had little effect on stoppages. Using a dry lubricant decreased reports of stoppages only for the M4 users. However, soldiers using a non-Army issued lubricant were more likely to have confidence in the reliability of their weapon. (Russell 2006: 32)

There are several important points contained in these two paragraphs. The opening sentence, for example, makes it clear that weapon stoppages were a generally common occurrence during firefights across the weapon types. Every weapon, even those with particularly good reputations for reliability, will jam at some point. Most of these stoppages are, of course, relatively minor, requiring little more than use of the charging handle to clear, but far more substantial stoppages do occur, demanding that the operator perform time-consuming and intricate stoppage procedures, particularly if the weapons have been hard used. The key point, of course, is the *frequency* of the stoppages, and the relative levels of seriousness of each stoppage. Suffice to say for now that there will always be reports of troops having weapon stoppages at moments of maximum mortal inconvenience, without diminishing the seriousness of those reports.

The second paragraph of the quotation almost appears to make a counterintuitive point, namely that diligent weapon cleaning is not important. Data presented later in the article demonstrates that this is not the case, however. Rather, the report found that there was no difference in the levels of weapon stoppages between those troops who performed a complete "tear down" of the weapon once a week or every day. This analysis does seem like it needs additional context, especially regarding the relationship between combat usage and levels of cleaning. The key point, however, seems to be that no extraordinary levels of cleaning or maintenance were required to keep the weapons functional in theater. Another point of interest in the quotation above includes the note that "firing in semi-automatic mode resulted in positive effects," including a more reliable performance. This is not to say that troops should treat the full-auto option on their carbines as something of a luxury that they should only be used sparingly, but the laws of physics apply to all firearms; controlled semi-auto fire will always be a more reliable mode that full-auto fire.

In the discussion about the M4s reliability, we should also acknowledge that weapon reliability in general is not just a matter of the weapon's core design. Human factors such as maintenance routines and the quality of crucial externals – particularly magazines and ammunition – all contribute to the reliability profile of a weapon. In these regards, Russell's report noted that:

Qualification level and soldier training did not have an effect on reported stoppages. However, confidence in weapon reliability was higher for soldiers in upper qualification levels. Soldiers who had trained with the weapon in an environment similar to theater prior to deployment were also more likely to be confident in the reliability of their weapon.

More usage of the weapon (defined as reported amount of ammunition used) increased the odds of weapons needing repair while

US Navy personnel fire M4s configured for CQB during basic combat marksmanship training. Note how the operators have installed custom magazine wells, the flared lower portion facilitating rapid reloads. (US Navy photo by Mass Communication Specialist 1st Class Joseph W. Pfaff/Released/Wikimedia/Public Domain)

in theater. Weapons that were rebuilt were also reportedly repaired more often than non-rebuilt weapons, and those with rebuilt weapons were less likely to be confident in the durability of the weapon. For all four weapon types, soldiers requested weapons and ammunition with more stopping power/lethality. Soldiers also recommended higher quality magazines for the M9, M4, and M16; more durable ammunition belt links and drum systems; and reduced size and weight in the M16 and M249. (Russell 2006: 33)

For the M4/M4A1 and M16, the issue of magazines has been central, as magazine quality, or lack of it, has accounted for a high percentage of mechanical issues. Up to 2009, the 5.56mm NATO STANAG magazine used in the M16 and the M4/M4A1 was manufactured to the most economical standards, using very lightweight metals and plastics for the magazine body, followers, and springs. These magazines were largely treated as one-use disposable items in front-line use, but they were also prone to damage, rust, and other environmental effects, with consequent tendencies to misfeed rounds or jam up. Following the adverse battlefield reports, the US military made a series of improvements to the rifle and carbine magazines, particularly focusing on making strong, more corrosion-resistant springs and introducing an improved anti-tilt follower. The US military also began to use commercial magazines produced from high-quality materials (including impact-resistant polymer bodies), some with more advanced features such as viewing panels so the operator can see at a glance how many rounds are left in the magazine.

Before drawing the threads of the M4/M4A1 reliability discussion together, we must also briefly examine one of the most negative assessments of the M4's reliability, namely the 2007 Aberdeen Rifle Dust Tests, conducted at Aberdeen Proving Ground, Maryland. The tests were launched when the M4 was the subject of some intense political and media scrutiny over its reliability, particularly in relation to claims that

A US soldier of the 101st Airborne Division carefully cleans out the receiver of his M4 carbine. He will remove not only dust, but also the buildup of brass and copper particles deposited during the firing cycle. (Mario Tama/ Getty Images)

the M4 was highly prone to stoppages caused by dust intrusion, of the type commonly experienced in Iraq and Afghanistan. The Aberdeen Rifle Dust Tests consisted of taking ten of each of four 5.56mm weapons – M4 carbine, XM8, HK 416, and MK16 (the M4 was the only direct-impingement weapon) – and firing 6,000 rounds through each weapon, putting it through an extreme dust immersion chamber every 120 rounds, with full clean and relubrication every 1,200 rounds. The total number of stoppages for each weapon type were then aggregated.

The results of this test were, at first glance, quite damning for the M4. The stoppages listed below (adapted from US Army 2007: Slide 6) are those per 60,000 rounds per weapon system (a Class 1 stoppage is a failure to feed/failure to fire; a Class 2 stoppage is a failure to eject; a Class 3 stoppage is a double feed):

TEST PERIOD	MALFUNCTION CLASS/ WEAPON	CLASS 1 & 2 WEAPON STOPPAGES	CLASS 1 & 2 MAGAZINE STOPPAGES	TOTAL CLASS 1 & 2 STOPPAGES	TOTAL CLASS 3 STOPPAGES
Summer 2007	M4 Test 2	148	148	296	11
Fall 2007	M4 Test 3	624	239	863	19
	XM8	98	18	116	11
	HK 416	210	9	219	14
	MK16	191	19	210	16

Just a cursory glance through the findings demonstrates a massive disparity in the levels of stoppages when the M4 is compared to the other weapons. This test was pounced upon by some as evidence that the M4 was not fit for purpose. Others, however – troops, statisticians, and firearms experts – have seriously questioned both the methodology and the results of the test.

The analysis is complex, but there are some salient points alleged. First, the M4s used in the trials were off-the-rack weapons with older serial numbers, while many of the other weapons were brand-new firearms built in anticipation of the tests. We are not aware of the condition of the M4 magazines, but that could also have been highly significant. The dust immersion levels were truly extreme, and not representative of real theater conditions. There have also been allegations that the trial operators were not familiar with the M4's three-round-burst mechanism, and were occasionally counting a failure to reset as a stoppage (although the author has been unable to confirm this). Most significant, why the major difference in results between the summer and fall tests? This suggests that the test was not repeatable with consistent results – one of the key requirements for test validation. Thus the use of the Aberdeen Rifle Dust Tests certainly raises a point of reflection as to the M4's reliability, but they are arguably not a definitive benchmark by which to judge the weapon's fitness for purpose.

If we were to try to find a resolution to the M4/M4A1 reliability debate, we can point to a comment of one soldier from *The Washington Times* report, who said that the M4 wasn't a bad weapon per se, just one needing improvements. Since the key years of the controversy (*c.*2005–07), the M4/M4A1 has been hugely improved on numerous levels. The M4 was never designed to provide almost the same levels of firepower as a light machine gun, so using it as a de facto LMG we could reasonably expect failures. As Colt and the US military became aware of how the weapon was actually being used in combat, however, they responded with incremental modifications to the M4A1 that have produced a respected weapon. Certainly, for every adverse opinion of the M4/M4A1, I seem to come across a contrastingly positive perspective on the weapon. The M4/M4A1 is not perfect, indeed, but the question is always, is it good enough to deserve the trust of the troops who now carry it? To that question, I would suggest that with all the improvements in barrel, trigger mechanism, magazines, and a multitude of other elements, there is enough evidence to say that it is. The following data is adapted from Russell's report (Russell December 2006: 30):

SOLDIER RECOMMENDATIONS FOR THE M4 FROM THE 2006 CAN SURVEY		
Descriptor	**% of M4 users**	**Recommendations**
Bullet	20%	Larger-caliber bullet
		Increase stoppage – lethality
Magazine	10%	Improve quality
		Larger capacity
		See-through magazine
General	8%	Replace weapon
		Too much noise – request silencer
		Increase range of weapon
Ammunition packaging	6%	Include loading system
		Make more secure/durable
Ammunition type	5%	Request hollow-point
		Request armor-piercing
Element susceptibility	5%	Too much maintenance
		Too susceptible to elements

AMMUNITION AND LETHALITY

A final area of debate regarding the M4/M4A1 is its performance in terms of lethality and range. In many ways, this is an argument about what is the most effective caliber of ammunition to use in a modern combat rifle, rather than about the M4/M4A1 itself. This is a rather sprawling and intense discussion that I won't explore in full here. To give the bare bones of the argument, however, some authorities claim that the 5.56×45mm round falls short in terms of range, penetration, and terminal effect, especially when fired from a shorter-barrel weapon such the M4/M4A1. These authorities often go on to advocate a shift to a heavier standard caliber, such as 6.5mm or 6.8mm or even back to 7.62mm. Others have countered that the 5.56×45mm round is fine as a general-purpose infantry round, especially fired from a weapon that has advanced optics to enable improved shot placement over range.

The debate is one of the most complex in modern firearms, involving a heavy dose of internal, external, and terminal ballistics. I do believe there is a case for a heavier round, but here I will reflect more upon the ballistic differences between the M4/M4A1 and the full-length M16 rifle and what improvements in 5.56×45mm ammunition mean for the performance of the carbine on the battlefield. From battlefield feedback, however, the main concerns about the M4/M4A1's performance are threefold: inadequate stopping power, with enemy combatants still functioning and fighting after having been hit by several rounds of 5.56×45mm; inadequate range, with the M4/M4A1 struggling to engage enemy troops over distances roughly in excess of 500m (547yd), whereas enemies armed with 7.62mm weaponry appeared to have fewer issues with such medium-range engagements; and inadequate penetration, especially at ranges of more than 500m, at which the M4/M4A1's rounds could fail to penetrate basic physical barriers, such as walls, steel plate, and soldier-mounted equipment.

Some of these concerns we can partially explain by the discrepancy between expectation and reality. Regarding the stopping power issue, for example, Hollywood and TV action films typically show a person dropping down dead immediately after being hit by a bullet. In reality, such an instant death from gunshot wounds almost never happens; instead the victim succumbs to blood-volume shock or other systematic failures over a period of time, ranging from a few seconds to many minutes or even hours, during which interval they can often remain combat active. This is why most firearms authorities agree that while caliber is important, accurate shot placement on the target (i.e. into areas of the body that will produce the most critical effects) is more so.

There are also genuine technical issues to address, however. Over the past decades, one of the main critiques of the M4/M4A1's ballistic performance relates to the drop in velocity resulting from using a barrel measuring 14.5in or less. From the 1980s, a pioneer of modern terminal ballistics, Dr. Martin Fackler, demonstrated that a central ingredients of a bullet's wounding effect is the fragmentation or yaw it undergoes once it passes into the human body. Fragmentation – in which the bullet shatters into multiple parts – is especially important, as it increases the area of the

"permanent cavity" within the body, accelerating the blood-volume shock. The likelihood of fragmentation is increased with velocity, and Fackler noted that with the introduction of carbine-length AR-15s the shortened barrels dropped the velocity of the round, decreasing the likelihood of its fragmentation on hitting the target. Instead, such rounds are more likely to simply penetrate through in a clean path, imposing far less incapacitation upon the target.

The issue of underperforming 5.56×45mm rounds, when fired from carbines, has since the 1980s received substantial analysis, galvanized in the 2000s by the exponential increase in the distribution of the M4/M4A1 to troops in Iraq and Afghanistan. The principal round fired by the majority of US troops in these theaters is the 62-grain M855/SS109. The ideal fragmentation velocity of this round – with some considerable variation owing to a variety of environmental factors – is about 2,500ft/sec. Tests indicate that in laboratory trial conditions, the M16A2 maintains this threshold out to 190m (208yd), while for the M4 that drops to 125m (137yd). Under more realistic field conditions, firing from well-used weapons and with the ammunition under colder temperatures, the figures drop to about 133m (145yd) for the M16A2 and just 66m (72yd) for the M4 (Nathaniel F. 2016). So, it does appear that the M4/M4A1, firing the M855 cartridge, has something of a problem within its terminal ballistics. The extent of this problem also changes on a round-for-round basis with yaw, i.e. the rotation of the bullet tip around the axis of flight. If the bullet strikes the target at the moment when yaw presents the tip of the bullet significantly off-center, the effects of the bullet on the target will be greater, as the yaw will increase bullet tumbling and fragmentation. If, however, the bullet enters the target dead straight (or nearly so), and at below the fragmentation threshold, then the bullet

US soldiers with 3d Platoon, Alpha Company, 1st Battalion, 503d Infantry Regiment, 173d Airborne Brigade Combat Team, prepare to engage enemy combatants in Chak district, Wardak Province, Afghanistan, 2010. While one man is armed with an M4 plus M203 underbarrel grenade launcher, the other two have far greater reach with their 7.62×51mm Mk 14 Enhanced Battle Rifles. (Pfc. Donald Watkins/US Army/Wikimedia/Public Domain)

might either simply pass through or become arrested in the target at the end of a slender permanent cavity. (There are huge variables here, such as the effects on the bullet path if it passes through thick webbing straps.) In service, US and Coalition troops also noted that the M855 often struggled to pass through basic enemy body armor, if it was worn.

The issues with the M855 are not absolute, and troops can compensate through accurate shot placement – something the M4/M4A1 is very good at – with the right sights and in the hands of a competent shooter. Nevertheless, some units decided that a better round was needed. During the early 2000s, for example, SOCOM changed to using the Mk 262, a 77-grain open-tip match round with much-improved terminal ballistics. Wanting even better performance, however, in around 2005 NSWC-Crane began development of another 5.56×45mm round, which has the same weight as the M855 but with an improved penetrator and the tip of the Mk 262. This round emerged as the Mk 318 Special Operations Science and Technology (SOST) cartridge, and it became the replacement for the Mk 262 in SOCOM.

Other services were taking note of the SOCOM policies. The US Marine Corps in particular made a partial adoption of the Mk 262 then a full adoption of the Mk 318 SOST. The US Army was also aware of the issues with the M855, and from the early 2000s had been developing its own more effective 5.56×45mm round, led by research from the Joint Services Wound Ballistics Integrated Product Team (JSWB IPT). The new cartridge that was developed, called the M855A1, emerged in 2010. It has a 62-grain projectile with an exposed steel-tipped penetrator and a copper core (there is no lead in the bullet), and it thus achieves a high degree of penetration, including against body armor. The Army also optimized the pressure of the cartridge for the M4/M4A1, closing the gap in muzzle velocities between the carbine and the full-length M16 rifle, and lowered the fragmentation threshold, likely down to the region of 1,900ft/sec. Fired from an M4/M4A1, therefore, the round's fragmentation threshold would be more around 326m (357yd), which is superior to that of an M16A2 firing a standard M855.

The improvement of 5.56×45mm ammunition is just another of the evolutionary advances the M4/M4A1 has made over the last 30 years. Concluding an assessment of the weapon's impact, it is clear that the M4/M4A1 has been exposed to a level of sudden battlefield testing few other modern weapons have undergone. This experience has revealed some flaws and limitations, as it has in other weapon systems, but most of these have been addressed in subsequent improvements. We might also add the question: what if the M4/M4A1 had not been available? Battles in Iraq and Afghanistan have largely been conducted via small-unit actions, often inside buildings or on narrow streets, in which firearms have played a leading role. The M4/M4A1 gave US and some Coalition forces a weapon that was ideally suited to MOUT and short- to medium-range firefights, and for use from or within the helicopters and infantry fighting vehicles that provide much of the combat transportation. In many ways, we can say that the M4/M4A1 was the right weapon at the right time.

CONCLUSION

Of one thing we can be certain – the M4/M4A1 carbine will be with us for many years to come. This being said, we are already witnessing the next stages of weapon evolution, and indeed the future generation of weapons that could eventually replace the M4/M4A1 as a standard-issue military firearm. Piston-driven weapons such as the HK 416 point toward the future replacement of the M4 in US military service. At the time of writing, however, other potential contenders are coming from the Next Generation Squad Weapons (NGSW) program, an endeavor to secure if not replacements then at least alternatives for the M4A1, M249, and M240B, potentially by 2023.

There is still some fight left in the M4/M4A1 for the future. A recent development known as the "M4A1+" is a range of modifications intended to upgrade the M4A1's capabilities and ergonomics. Some of the elements available or under development include: an extended forward rail; a free-floating barrel; an improved flash suppressor; an optional sniper-quality single-stage trigger (a single-stage trigger releases the shot as soon as it is moved, while a two-stage trigger has a range of movement or "slack" before the shot); an advanced fire-control system featuring target tracking, environmental sensors, automatic ballistic calculation, heads-up display, and information networking; and a no-fire weapon zeroing device. With such modifications, and others, the M4A1 may well endure far longer than some have predicted.

In the US military, the expectation is that the M4/M4A1 carbines and M16 rifles will only be replaced once there is a fundamental step forward in technology that makes the investment worthwhile. It remains to be seen whether the NGSW program is that step forward, or whether the M4A1's modularity and ongoing modifications can keep the carbine in the front line.

An M4 carbine, without the optional carrying handle and fitted with the RAS front rail. The fire selector indicator on the side is an easy way to identify the M4 from an M4A1; the word "BURST" indicates the three-round-burst feature of the M4. (Photo courtesy of PEO Soldier/Wikimedia/Public Domain)

BIBLIOGRAPHY

3d Infantry Division (Mechanized) (July 2003). *Third Infantry Division (Mechanized) After Action Report: Operation IRAQI FREEDOM*. Fort Stewart, GA: 3d Infantry Division.

Burden, Matthew Currier (2006). *The Blog of War: Front-line Dispatches from Soldiers in Iraq and Afghanistan*. New York, NY: Simon & Schuster.

Defense Security Cooperation Agency (n.d.). Definition of "technical data package." Accessed at: https://samm.dsca.mil/glossary/technical-data-package-tdp

Defense Security Cooperation Agency (2008). "News Release." December 10, 2008. Accessed at: https://www.dsca.mil/major-arms-sales/iraq-m16a4-rifles-m4-carbines-and-m203-grenade-launchers

Department of Defense (1997). *Audit Report: Procurement of M4 Carbines*. Washington, DC: Office of the Inspector General, Department of Defense.

Feickert, Andrew (2010). *The Army's M-4 Carbine: Background and Issues for Congress*. Washington, DC: Congressional Research Service.

Kim, Sung Y. (2006). "5.56mm Reduced Ricochet Limited Penetration (RRLP), Mk 255 Mod 0." Crane, IN: Small Arms Ammunition Branch Crane Division, Naval Surface Warfare Center.

Mizokami, Kyle (2019). "M4 Carbine: this rifle is so good that the U.S. Army can't lose a shootout." *The National Interest*, November 15, 2019.

Nathaniel F. (2016). "Long Barrel, or Short? The Effectiveness Trade-Off Between 14.5" and 20" Barrels." The Firearms Blog. Accessed at: https://www.thefirearmblog.com/blog/2016/11/23/long-barrel-short-fragmentation-threshold-trade-off-14-5-20-barrels/

Office of Inspector General (1997). *Audit Report: Procurement of M4 Carbines*. Washington, DC: Department of Defense.

PEO Soldier (2012). "M4 Carbine Product Improvement Program (PIP) Update." Accessed at: http://peosoldier.armylive.dodlive.mil/2012/08/23/m4-carbine-product-improvement-program-pip-update/

Rottman, Gordon L. (2011). *The M16*. Weapon 14. Oxford: Osprey Publishing.

Russell, Sara M. (2006). *Soldier Perspectives on Small Arms in Combat*. Alexandria, VA: CAN.

Scales, Robert H. (2015). "Gun Trouble." *The Atlantic*. January/February 2015. Accessed at: https://www.theatlantic.com/magazine/archive/2015/01/gun-trouble/383508/

Scarborough, Rowan (2014a). "Troops left to fend for themselves after Army was warned of flaws in rifle." *The Washington Times*,

February 19, 2014. Accessed at:
https://www.washingtontimes.com/news/2014/feb/19/troop-left-
to-fend-for-themselves-after-army-was-w/

Scarborough, Rowan (2014b). "Cover-up? Army historian says report
on deadly Afghan battle was altered to absolve faulty gun," *The
Washington Times*, February 20, 2014. Accessed at: https://m.
washingtontimes.com/news/2014/feb/20/cover-up-army-
historian-says-report-on-deadly-afgh/

Schehl, Matthew L. (2015). "Marine grunts react to switch from the
M16 to the M4," *Marine Corps Times*, November 1, 2015.
Accessed at: https://www.marinecorpstimes.com/news/your-
marine-corps/2015/11/01/marine-grunts-react-to-switch-from-
the-m16-to-the-m4/

Small Arms Solutions (2018a). "The History of the M4." Accessed at:
https://www.youtube.com/watch?v=7Td20TRQWK0

Small Arms Solutions (2018b). "The History of the M4 – Part 2."
Accessed at: https://www.youtube.com/watch?v=zHo9z_
C0Du0US Army (1991). TM 9-1005-319-23&P, *Unit and Direct
Support Maintenance Manual (Including Repair Parts and Special
Tools List) For RIFLE, 5.56MM, M16A2,
W/E(1005-01-128-9936) CARBINE, 5.56MM, M4 (1005-01-
231-0973) AND CARBINE, 5.56MM, M4A1 (1005-01-382-
0953)*. Washington, DC: Departments of the Army and Air Force.

US Army (2003). *Rifle Marksmanship M16A1, M16A2/3, M16A4, and
M4 Carbine*. Washington, DC: Headquarters, Department
of the Army.

US Army (2007). Carbine Extreme Dust Test (PPT). Aberdeen
Proving Ground.

US Army (2013). Press release, June 13, 2013. Accessed at:
https://soldiersystems.net/2013/06/13/breaking-army-concludes-
individual-carbine-competition-without-winner/

US Army (2016). *Rifle and Carbine*. Washington, DC: Department
of the Army.

US Army CSI (2010). *Wanat: Combat Action in Afghanistan, 2008*. Fort
Leavenworth, KS: Combat Studies Institute Press.

Watters, Daniel E. (2011). "Colt M4 Data Rights & The Individual
Carbine Competition." *Defense Industry Daily* online, June 21,
2011. Accessed at: https://www.defenseindustrydaily.com/Colt-
M4-Data-Rights-The-Individual-Carbine-Competition-06942/

Wood, Keith (2013). "G&A Perspectives: Do We Need the AR-15
Forward Assist?" *Guns & Ammo* online, November 5, 2013.
Accessed at: https://www.gunsandammo.com/editorial/ga-
perspectives-need-ar-15-forward-assist/249766

INDEX